T0128195

# The Art
# Of Transformation

## A Daily Approach
## To Uplifting Your Life

NOELLE BOVON

**BALBOA.**
PRESS

A DIVISION OF HAY HOUSE

Balboa Press books may be ordered through booksellers or by contacting:

Balboa Press
A Division of Hay House
1663 Liberty Drive
Bloomington, IN 47403
www.balboapress.com
1 (877) 407-4847

Print information available on the last page.

ISBN: 978-1-9822-3038-8 (sc)
ISBN: 978-1-9822-3039-5 (e)

Balboa Press rev. date: 11/14/2019

# Contents

# Gratitude

I have the privilege to write and to do the work I am doing because of all the courageous women and men who have come before me. However, I want to dedicate this book to all the exceptional women who have forged the path ahead of me.

For the women who took risks, who never saw anyone else do what they dreamed of and who found the courage to become what they wanted to be.

For the women, whether they are politicians, economists, thought leaders, story tellers, explorers, rule breakers, scientists, mothers, writers, entrepreneurs, creators, artists or activists, who are able to articulate unpopular truths in a way that others can digest.

For the ones seen and unseen: the ones who have forged ahead when it was dangerous to speak their truth and those who lost their lives to make changes for equality.

For my daughter, Reese. I love you more than I could have ever imagined possible. My journey of healing is so that you may have an opportunity to brave the world without having to first heal yourself from the traumas of our lineage. I want you to have the privilege of knowing you are loved and supported in all that you choose to take on in the world.

For my mother, who lived a life filled with pain and shame. She struggled yet always did the best she could. She carried a lot of pain, but I know she is now free of that pain. You loved us in all ways and always believed in us. To my father, who also left the world way too early. You and I had a beautiful connection as adults, and I miss you. You both gave me the life that I am meant to live and for that I am so grateful.

Finally, to my sisters and three nieces: Anne, Michelle, Malin, Emmy and Isla. You bring so much pleasure to my life. I wish you brilliant lives and the ability to feel love in a way that is bigger than anything you have felt up until now.

To the known and unknown women in our world, I bow to your bravery and willingness to show up in your lives. To the women who have influenced me in person or with their work: Dr. Maya Angelou, Dr. Brené Brown, Elizabeth Gilbert, Oprah Winfrey, Louise Hay, Sean Corn, Dr. Christine Northrup and

Kate Northrup, Marie Forleo, Ally Bogard, Karuna Erikson, Sister Joan Chittister, Dr. Shafali Tsabary, Marianne Williamson, Caroline Myss, Cheryl Strayed, Tara Brach, Esther Perel and the many other amazing women who have been profound influences in my life.

Namaste

# Opening

'Transformation' is a bold word. It alludes to change or a full shift. But what exactly does it take to make a full transformation or to change your life? I have never believed myself to be an expert; however, I have a lot of life experience. My views are not new, but the way I have lived my life is unique to me. No one else has my stories or life map, just as no one else has lived your life or journeyed as you have.

I have used my writing to help create connection. I was lost in my struggles for so many years; lost in myself and in my traumas. My struggles gave me a lot of skills, but eventually I found that I needed to evolve out of my struggles and become the person I am meant to be. I took charge of my life and my emotional well-being. I started this path years ago, but the moment

I asked my husband for a divorce was the moment I finally learned to step into myself. The separation was a gruelling process and I felt lonely and isolated. I was terrified of what my future would look like and of the struggles I would endure as I moved through leaving my ex. I knew that I needed to create a life that felt kind and loving. This was something I had not yet experienced, but I understood it was a possibility.

I wanted to create a home that I would be proud to raise my daughter in and invite friends and loved ones to visit. A home that was filled with love; a place that was healthy and safe for me to be me. I wanted a stable home for my daughter to able to be courageous in love and life, feel a sacred connection to our house and build strength in herself. I have accomplished that: our home is our sanctuary. In the midst of our full lives we have a place to land and feel supported.

This book is unique in that it is designed to be digested in small doses. I want you to be able to pick it up and consume the chapter that feels most relevant to you on any given day. Or you can use it as a daily guide to choosing to showing up for yourself. It might be the tool you need to unpack your day and explore the ways you want to celebrate who you are. It may allow you to find a deeper connection to the workings of your mind. However, it is also a book you can discuss with your partner or use in a book club with your friends, something that gives you direction as you learn to open up about your processes.

I got tired of living a life built on feeling shame and guilt and projecting blame outward. I hope my writing helps you embrace who you are, without feelings of shame or guilt. Remember that your story is unique to you, as mine is to me. I share my stories only so that I can put words to the experiences we all have and create connection so that we may understand we are not alone. In a world that is promoting social behaviours that seem to create more isolation, my goal is to initiate connection through honest dialogue.

I live for honest conversations because being truthful creates intimacy and love for one another. I strive to create a conscious community built on uniqueness rather than divisiveness. I aim to have conversations about healing my unhealthy responses and behaviours so that collectively we all find the courage to do so individually. As we learn to build strong foundations we can make healthy changes in our relationships and, in turn, in the world. When we heal and have honest conversations we create space for those around us to work through their own struggles. Our goal should not be to try to change someone, but to support them. I have learned that when I am supported, I can do my work. When I feel like someone is trying to change me or if I feel judged for having my own experience, it takes longer for me to evolve and grow.

My life has evolved and I have grown and changed. I continue to evolve and be brave in my life. I am learning to be open with my heart and I have softened a great deal. I understand that my softening is not a weakness, but a strength. I want you to know that as you move through the processes you need for your evolution, you are exactly where you need to be in this moment for your soul and your emotional growth.

Please don't render your process to judgement because you need to find your path, your truth; at times it will not be graceful, you will fail, you will fall and you will struggle and suffer. But trust that without those experiences you will not get to where you need to be.

Perfection is a myth when we expect it of others and of ourselves. May we find the courage to be imperfect, to be less than someone else, to be OK being flawed and to allow those feelings as much authority as those that feel good. Those feelings help remind us that we are human. It is important not to overindulge in negative feelings, but as important not to push them away. We are not meant to feel happy all the time. We are meant to experience emotion in all forms and it is what we do with these emotions and how we respond to our mind and body and to others that matters most. When we learn to be grounded in our emotions regardless of what comes up, we give others permission to have their own emotions. That in itself is transformative.

I have learned to be patient and stop storming through my life. I hope this book helps you find more patience with yourself and evolve in ways that you may have never expected. I am constantly learning to let go of certainty; when I let the world show up without needing to control it, I experience moments of magic all the time.

Use this book of transformation with a willing heart and be kind to yourself. This being human is big work. It takes bravery to show up and do our work and we won't get anywhere if we expect life to be 'perfect' or if we avoid challenge. This book can help you make changes that bring about more peace, but the journey of evolution will bring up triggers, inner conflicts and challenging times. I want you to know that it's OK: it is OK to be challenged and OK to be moved to tears or to your knees.

Surround yourself with people that support you for being you, and stop giving your precious time to those who don't. It is a simple sentiment to share, but not necessarily simple to live or learn. Most importantly, remember that you are worthy of receiving love and of living the life you want to live.

*Namaste*
*The light within me honours the light within you*
*All that is good within me sees all that is*
*good within you*

My hope is that you can see all that is good within you, because the degree of goodness or kindness or love we feel for ourselves is the amount we are able to feel for others. When we heal ourselves we heal the world. It is a privilege to be able to do our inner explorations. Even when you are in the trenches of your work, know that you are doing your part in becoming who you want to be. Trust that the light always come through the dark times.

# 1
# What Is Mindfulness?

Our life is shaped by our mind,
for we become what we think.
Gautama Buddha

After years of self-work, inner evolution and dramatic changes that have allowed me to feel more balanced in my emotions and self-worth, I decided my purpose was to share these transformative experiences, thoughts, ideas and actions so others would feel like they were not alone.

Mindfulness is the act of connecting consciously to your thoughts, behaviours and beliefs.

What does it mean to be mindful? Is mindfulness a way to achieve greatness or is it the antidote to suffering?

Self-awareness tunes us to mindfulness. A very simple definition of the meaning of mindfulness is "the quality or state of being conscious or aware of something". To break that down even more, mindfulness means to be aware of **ourselves** and the ways in which we interact in the world.

I believe we spend too much time thinking about what everyone else is doing and not enough time thinking about what we are doing. Where are you directing your attention and thoughts? What stories play over and over again in your mind?

When you start to pay attention to the ways you interact with the world, you enter the realm of mindfulness. You begin to unravel the webs of confusion in your life related to your work, your relationships with others and, most profoundly, your relationship with yourself.

There are so many things to pay attention to. My challenge for you is to start with your breath. Notice how your breath feels. Notice what happens in your body when you pay attention to it. Does it feel good? Does it calm you down? Do you become more distracted, or more focused? Just notice. It is that simple.

I want you to know that your biggest learning exists right inside of you. Your breath is your biggest teacher. As simple as that sounds, it is one hundred percent true.

Mindfulness will give you the tools to notice what causes your suffering. What you do with that awareness is the light switch that affects being tuned in or turned off.

When we are mindful, we are not judging ourselves; mindfulness is about being compassionate to our own journey as we learn to pay attention. It is the ability to be aware of our actions and responses in the world. Mindfulness is being gentle and kind, but fierce with compassion. It is about being unwavering at times. Mindfulness is remembering who you are in your heart and holding that awareness above anyone's ideals. It is choosing **how you are going to respond to any given situation** throughout each day and choosing when to respond with either kindness, assertiveness or fierceness.

Mindfulness is knowing that **everyone** is on their own path, and that choosing to be mindful in no way denotes that others should respond accordingly. It's about understanding that each and every day you will be met with small and big challenges. Yet in each and every moment you get to choose how to respond. Just because you choose to respond by fiercely setting boundaries in one encounter does not mean you have to respond the same way the next moment. You can choose to move from kindness and gentleness.

Mindfulness is letting go of self-judgment when we have not responded well, and doing the same for others.

Being mindful does not mean you have all the answers. It does not mean you have to get it right all the time.

It means that you are aware of the intricacy of the ebb and flow of your emotions, of others people's emotions and of learning to navigate each situation a little different.

Mindfulness is letting go. It is letting go of our attachments, our need to know outcomes and our desire to have things go a certain way. Letting go is a monumental statement to yourself – it is no longer moving from a place of forcing but from a willingness to be present in whatever happens. It doesn't mean you become a doormat or that you don't have dreams and desires. It means that you stop being in a constant state of resistance.

Mindfulness is breathing in conscious thoughts and reactions every single day. **It is a lifelong practice**. The more we do it, the better we get at watching ourselves. However, we are not superior for being mindful, and being mindful does not mean we control others to get what we want. We do, however, get better at creating better outcomes for ourselves because we no longer expect certainty. We begin to understand that life is a constant balancing act of our desires and the desires of everyone else.

Being mindful is being passionately gentle and fiercely aware. It is balancing primitive, ingrained responses with a heavy dose of observation.

Will you choose to be observant today? Take it one moment at a time and something will arise that is worth paying attention to.

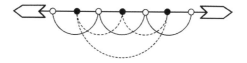

# JOURNAL

At the end of this chapter you will find a section for journaling. This is a guidepost to use in future chapters, I do recommend you have your own journal to track your answers and thoughts in each chapter. The purpose is to give you time to process each chapter and make notes so you can remember your 'ah-ha' moments and process your thoughts about the chapter.

It's worth finding someone you can share your progress with, an 'accountability partner' (perhaps a friend who is reading this book as well). It is ideal to have someone you can call when you are feeling challenged and need support as well as someone who can celebrate your successes.

Who is my accountability partner? When I am feeling challenged and I need support, I can reach out to:

---

I use some language in the journal section that is vague; the purpose of that language is to create a creative space where you can process. In the journal section I also speak about patience a great deal.

Patience can present in several different ways: how we respond to ourselves, how we respond to others, how we allow for imperfection and how we give ourselves time to process any given topic, idea or thought. We play out patience with the dialogue in our minds. When we are unkind it can sound like: "Why don't I do this already?", "What is wrong with me?", "Why can't I get this quicker?", "Why is this so hard?", "Everyone does this better." When patience is kind it can sound like: "I've got this.", "This is hard, but I am going to be fine.", "Look at all the positive things I have already accomplished in my life.".

Patience takes practice. There is always a visceral sensation you get when you are feeling impatient. How does impatience feel in your body? If you are able to identify this, you will be able to more quickly translate the emotions that come up because you will already understand the sensations associated with the feelings.

Another piece of language I use in the journal section is 'showing up". Showing up refers to the different ways we support ourselves and others in any situation that presents. It can translate into 'self-care' or how you prioritize your health in a physical and emotional way. It allows you to question whether you get the amount of exercise you need to feel healthy, consider how much time you want outside each day to feel connected to nature and value your nutrition, down time and a good night's sleep. Showing up also involves having clear boundaries with your time, work, obligations and friends. It means you surround yourself with people who allow you to be you and who allow for failure and provide compassion as you learn from your mistakes. I see setting clear boundaries as learning to create a healthy relationship with yourself. In turn, this manifests into creating healthy relationships with others. Boundaries can change and evolve, as you do. But learn to know your boundaries so that you can keep yourself accountable. You may want to write them down and have them posted in your bedroom so you can be reminded of them daily.

The journal section of this book is broken down at the end of the first chapter, it is an example of what to think about after each chapter that doesn't have specific questions. This book is more easily digested in short burst. Take your time and make notes as needed, which will help you process your thoughts as you evolve as a human. It is a personal and intimate way to get to know yourself. It will allow you to see who you are in this world, how you perceive what's happening around you and how things may or may not be working for you in any given topic. It's your opportunity to do your work. Instead of using this book as another way to consume mindful ideas, this allows you to take action and find ways to implement the lessons into your life.

I hope you are excited to move through this process. It has been transformative for me and today I am living a fulfilling life and have a healthy relationship with my family, friends and community. Most importantly, I have developed healthy habits of how I talk to myself and take care of myself.

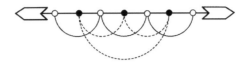

**Internal Commentary:**

What kinds of things do you say to yourself to show kindness and self-acceptance?

_____

_____

Do you find there is negative commentary running through your mind? How does this affect how you feel about yourself?

_____

_____

Are you patient with yourself as you process new ways of seeing things or new ways of showing up in your life? Note the ways you are patient with yourself as well as the ways you are struggling with this.

_____

_____

How are you able to show up for yourself?

_____

_____

What barriers are making it difficult to find patience? Is there shame or past stories of hurt that feel particularly present and challenge you to find a positive outcome?

_____

_____

What can you do to become more patient, loving and accepting of your process?

_____

_____

## Showing Up:

In what ways do you want to show up for yourself in your life?

_____

_____

_____

How are you currently showing up for yourself? Be specific:

_____

_____

_____

What are other ways you can feel supported? Name some other ways you could be more present in your life:

_____

_____

_____

## Bring the Work into Your COMMUNITY:

Does this practice change the way you could show up for the people in your life? Consider your family, friends, partners and colleagues.

_____

_____

_____

Thoughts:

_____

_____

_____

_____

_____

# 2
# Daily Practices That Changed My Life

If you get the inside right, the
outside will fall into place.
Eckhart Tolle

I assume you are reading this because you are
interested in leading a conscious life. You are
curious about yourself and how you interact in the
world. I also imagine that you are like me – someone
who realizes that sometimes we need some support as
we fumble through life.

I have done a lot of 'self-work' over the last two-plus
decades, and I remain a work in progress. I do not
claim to have all the answers and in no way do I

believe I have everything figured out. I recognize **life** *is the work* – this work is conscious – and conscious work will remain part of my practice until I leave this body of mine.

I have had some very challenging times over the last few years, times that have made me crumble and question if I have what it takes. It's during those times that I had to dive into my resources and use them to lift me up and remind myself that I do have 'what it takes' to find grace in the ungraceful times.

Help comes in many different forms. I have learned that a steady foundation of practice is one of the best ways to receive help. Here are the steps and practices I use regularly to keep me feeling sane when life feels a bit insane. These are all non-negotiable everyday practices for me. I may miss a day or two, but I always come right back to them. They are the tools I use to help me when I feel like I don't have it in me to deal with what is.

**Keep Good Company:** I have learned that who I keep around me affects my sense of peace, anxiety and confidence. Since I want to feel supported and loved, and I want to be able to offer that same love and support, I have become selective about whom I share my space with. It hasn't been an easy process, but it has been an incredibly healthy process.

**Meditation:** This practice keeps me sane and grounded. I get less tripped up in my own and others' dramas when I meditate. Even if I sit for 20 minutes and 18 of those minutes I have a unruly mind, I leave the meditation in a more calm and centred state.

**Positive Self Talk:** I pay attention to what I say to myself. If I am rambling on about how awful I am, I catch myself and stop as soon as I notice. I turn the language to something I want to hear. These are actual things that I say to myself: "I am capable of amazing things", "I love you", "I am at peace in this very moment", "I am supported and loved", "The universes is conspiring in my favor". I practice this every day.

**Smile & dance:** I smile to myself as much as I can. When I get too serious, I smile. When I get too worked up, I try to dance. Both of these practices instantly change my negative state and remind me things are far sweeter than they appear.

**Gratitude:** Every day I think about what I am grateful for and I write it down.

**Exercise & food:** I need to fill my body everyday with healthy food and exercise. I can't get out every day, but exercising many days a week, ideally four or five, keeps me in a sane mind and a healthy body. I struggle with feeding myself enough (not because I can't afford it, which is something that many people struggle with), but because I can easily find reasons to skip a meal. I practice staying nourished as it helps reduce my anxiety and gives me energy to get through the day with mental clarity.

**Lemon and Water:** First thing in the morning, before I consume anything else, I drink lemon with water. It's changed my digestion, my immunity and my clarity.

**Yoga:** My saving grace. It helps me connect to my physical body. It is where I truly started to develop a loving relationship with myself. I no longer practice asana (postures) everyday, but I do practice the other limbs of yoga.

**Positive Books and Podcasts:** I read and or listen to a podcast that lights me up and reminds me there is a bigger world out there. This motivates me to do my own work, whether it's in career, relationships, love, finances, science or education.

I hope this helps. We will all find our own practices and daily rituals that help bring peace and sanity. Practices that we rely on for inner balance. What are yours? What are some simple practices you are drawn to? Start experimenting to figure out what your non-negotiable daily practices will be.

# 3

# Become Your Inner Master

Life is really simple, but we insist
on making it complicated.
Confucius

Isn't it great to know that you have a choice in how today, and this week, will be for you? Do you know that you are the creator of your life? *You have choice in how your day goes.*

I spent years thinking the outcome of my life was due to my circumstances or to the other people in it. It was awful: I'd wake up every day not knowing that I had a choice.

I'd see others who were happy, successful and confident as having something I did not. I thought they must be gifted with something I didn't have – that I must look to them – and that they must have the answers. I thought I should value them and their opinions of me over my own ideas and feelings of myself...since they had that something that I couldn't find in myself.

I began to realize this was not the case.

At some blissful point, I realized the only thing those people had that I didn't was the **belief that they were worthy** of what they had achieved.

That was the turning point for me.

I want you to know you are worthy of your life, worthy of feeling good and being happy, worthy of the dreams you have. Most importantly, you are worthy of feeling the light that exists within you.

You are the master of your own life. The **moment** you stop looking outside yourself for the answers is the **moment** you will begin to find the answers within. Stop finding ways to distract yourself from yourself. Whether it is social media, work, housework, exercise, kids, food, gossip, or obsessions: a distraction is a distraction.

Once you stop focusing on distractions, it can feel overwhelmingly quiet. I used to be so overwhelmed with quiet that I would always drive with the radio on; every time an unwanted thought would pop into my head, I would change the radio station, as if it would change the channel of my mind, as if it would bring me peace from myself!

It felt terrifying to get quiet, as though I might implode with the thoughts spinning in my mind.

But I didn't implode. I learned to be quiet for moments at a time, and in these moments I found space. I was able to let go of the anxiety that the thoughts created and find ease.

Here are three ways to help you find your Inner Master:

1) Sit quietly for two to five minutes (or even two to three breaths) and listen to what's happening for you. Do this every day, each day increasing the amount of time you get quiet and listen.
2) Pay attention to what feels good inside of you. Seriously, what feels good? Can you find where that space is located in your body? If so, hang out there for a few minutes (or breaths). If you can't find it, just keep trying, each day, each week, each month.
3) What happens inside of you when you pay attention? Write it down.

I hope this helps get you excited to look inward. To understand that **you** are your Inner Master. That once you stop looking outside of yourself, you'll begin to find 'amazingness' right inside you. That everything you need already exists within you. Trust me.

# 4

# You Have Only This Moment

Most humans are never really present
in the now, because unconsciously they
believe that the next moment must be more
important than this one. But then you
miss your whole life, which is never not
now. And that is a revelation for people,
to realize your life is only ever now.
Eckhart Tolle

It's **all** in this moment as your read these words
and feel what your mind and body are experiencing
**right now**.

You literally have only this **moment**. Nothing that has
happened in the past or that is coming in the future

exists right now. It is simply this exact breath and moment.

We spend most of our time considering past events, conflicts and journeys. Then we jump to planning for the future: work, groceries, house chores, children's schedules. Somewhere in there, you may be dreaming up ideas for future fun, adventures and your career.

But what about **right now**?

Have you been attentive enough to drink this moment in? This delicious, fine, everything-is-exactly-how-it-is-in-this-very-moment moment?

If you want to check your inner compass, if you want to connect in with what it feels like to be alive, to feel the air brush against your skin, it's **now**.

*Doesn't it feel good?*

It feels so good to know that you have this one moment. All the drama and stress in your life can still exist, but if you give them just a tiny pause, you can create space for your breath, your glorious, beautiful breath. Your breath is the one thing that carries you from moment to moment with absolutely unwavering commitment.

Try to instill as many moments of the **here** and **now** throughout your day as you can. See what happens, see what it feels like to unearth a deeper connection with incredible **you**.

I wish you a beautiful, pleasurable, exactly-as-it-should-be moment.

# 5

# Do You Allow Pleasure in Your Life?

Being vulnerable is the only way to
allow your heart to feel true pleasure.
Bob Marley

Pleasure, as defined by the *Oxford English Dictionary*, is "a feeling of happy satisfaction and enjoyment" (*OED*, n.1).
Synonyms: happiness, delight, joy, gladness, glee, satisfaction, gratification, contentment, amusement.

Do you invite pleasure into your life? How do you taste, experience and dance with pleasure? Does it seem too taboo to even think about in your life? What does pleasure mean to you?

Pleasure is the simple act of enjoying the little things in your life. Of finding joy and delight in living the small things that make up your life. However, I think we can only feel pleasure when we literaly feel pleasure in our body.

I think one way we can prevent pleasure, is sexually. There can be a lot of guilt and disconnection to our own innate feelings and gratification when we allow ourselves to be sexual beings. I believe, when we mute this part of ourselves it has a profound negative impact on our ability to live a pleasure filled life.

Do you feel guilty when you feel playful and enjoy just being you? Even the idea of enjoyment of being ourselves can feel foreign. Ask yourself why on earth it is worth feeling unsatisfied over feeling amazing? With our limited time on this earth, feeling good seems like a brilliant option.

Letting go of all the ways we convince ourselves that we should not enjoy pleasurable experiences opens us up to the thrill of even greater enjoyment. Giving ourselves permission to feel the amazing can also gift those around us the same privilege.

Bliss is something that we must allow into our lives today, it is not about the future. Stop saying that you'll be happy **when**...When we do that we are literally giving authority of our gratification over to a future moment and situation that is likely beyond our control.

Learn to revel in the moment. There are small things you can do everyday to bring more enjoyment into the life you are already living. Enjoy your time as you drink your coffee in the morning and make your way to work. Listen to the sounds and experience the smells along your everyday paths. Challenge yourself to notice new perspectives with friends. Look at your lover with the same glances that first attracted you. Invite in moments of enjoying the small things: the keyboard strikes under your fingertips, the sun shining brightly on your face. Delight in candid moments of awareness instead of seeing your life as a daily list of boxes to be checked.

You could even try saying "I **get** to..." instead of "I **have** to...."

Be the light. Move toward it with urgency. Let go of resistance. Find spirit in **all** moments. Let go of the pain, or at the very least, don't move away from it anymore. Find ways to love more, and to feel more en**JOY**ment in the little things.

Let go of the idea you don't deserve to feel good. Dabble in new ways of feeling all the feels that pleasure can coat us with.

There is so much pleasure to be had in this world, and you deserve all of it.

Trust in what you can't see

# 6

# Are You the Creator of Your Life?

If you don't spend the time making
the life you want, you're eventually
going to be forced to spend a lot of time
dealing with the life you don't want.
Kevin Ngo

Do you believe that your life circumstances make
you who you are? Have you surrendered your
dreams – or stopped dreaming altogether – because
you believe that what you have today is all you will
ever have?

When you consider your dreams, do you fill your mind
with excuses of why you are not capable of following

them? Do you consistently recite your stories as firm truths that justify why you are where you are? Are you someone who endlessly wonders why others have achieved amazing things in their lives, yet you can't?

Here is the thing: how can we be the **Creators of Our Lives** if we believe that what we have been given so far is all there can ever be?

Here is a little secret: your life story so far does not create your future **unless** you believe it does. Are you ready to create new experiences? Find the love of your life? Travel to a country you've always dreamed of? Explore a new career?

Have you made choices in your life because someone else has told you that you need to follow a certain path?

More importantly, do you know what you want? Do you even know who you are? Or what interests you? And if you can answer those questions, do you love yourself enough to move in the direction of your dreams, against whatever real or perceived resistance there may be?

It's hard to love a self you don't know or recognize. If the realization that this is your experience is scary, know that you're not alone. I connect with people over and over again that tell me they have no idea what they want, or what moves or inspires them.

Know this, too: *you are strong enough, brave enough, tough enough, kind enough and enough of everything else you need to make the life you want happen. Right now. This minute.*

So, my friend, what choice are you going to make **today** that is different than all the choices you have made up to this point?

The best way to get to Create the Life You Want is to do one thing differently than you did yesterday. Let yourself experience what you can't predict or imagine by acting even just a little bit outside of your habituated comfort zone. In doing so, you choose the unknown and position yourself to see what magic lies on the other side.

# 7
## Wake Up To Grace

Grace is the cousin to synchronicity.
Danielle Laporte

I wake up to grace every day the moment I realize I am still here. I am in control of this body of mine. I have choice in everything I do, and choice in how I respond to the world around me.

Waking up to grace doesn't involve angels singing or me floating through life, but it **does** mean that I wake up and think, "I have this day, so what am I going to do with it? How will I make it special?"

Most days, it includes making time for gratitude. I am grateful for my amazing little girl, for time to exercise, for my yoga practice, for time outside, for food on my table, for a roof over my head, for an amazing community of friends, and for a career I am blessed to have.

When I make time to feel grateful, grace seems to flow with abundance. I am more patient, more generous, more considerate, more caring, and more loving toward myself.

When I forget to find time for gratitude, I tend to be more rushed. I have a serious lack of patience, I blame others for my experiences, I am less forthcoming with my time and I forget how blessed I am to have all that I do in my life.

Those days are rude awakenings for me. They remind me that I have become absorbed in things that distract me from love and the grace of living.

It is because of this that those are days are also very important. They give me perspective, a mirror to remind myself that I have a choice: I can choose to travel down the dark road of despair, or I can choose to see the beauty around me.

Sometimes it takes me days to shake myself out of my own darkness – in the past it has taken me months or years – but when I do manage it, I find a lightness that chases out the shadows, and I remember how the simple practice of gratitude can always unfailingly wake me up to grace.

**So what are you grateful for today?**

Pay attention to all the moments of your day, even the ones that aren't so comfortable, and discover how a shift in perspective can lead you to feel grateful for all that you have created in your life. EVERYTHING can change.

Find your Grace.

# 8
## Does Being Vulnerable Scare You?

What makes you vulnerable
makes you beautiful.
Dr. Brené Brown

**B**eing vulnerable used to absolutely terrify me. Today I work diligently, consistently challenging myself to step into the discomfort of my vulnerability. Through this I find my inner strength.

I use the strength that exists within me to trust in my own instincts and to listen to the small quiet voice inside that is begging to be heard – the voice that pushes me to do things that scare me.

I do that by trusting that being vulnerable will not kill me. It is actually an inner compass of intelligence. When I allow vulnerability to be OK I am a far better version of myself.

When I am vulnerable, I take down walls instead of building more. I trust those around me instead of questioning their motives. I am gentler and kinder to myself and others.

To be clear, choosing to be vulnerable does not set you up to live without pain. But what it does do is help you open doors within yourself. It assists you with looking for acceptance inside yourself, instead of outside. It allows for a deeper sense of inner trust so that you can take risks you may have never imagined taking.

Starting my Mindful Mondays blog – that you are now reading – was/is a deeply vulnerable action for me. I couldn't give myself too much time to think about it or I would have convinced myself that putting myself out here like this would surely mean I would suffer great failure, rejection and embarrassment.

When I choose to be vulnerable I do it for myself, not for what others think. I trust deeply in my desire to serve others and follow my inner guidance so that I can be the person I am here to be. **'Whole', not perfect**.

# 9

## Do You Allow Others to
## Be Vulnerable?

Staying vulnerable is a risk we have to
take if we want to experience connection.
Dr. Brené Brown

In a recent a discussion with a friend, I articulated that I feel most people in my life do not allow me to be vulnerable. When I tuck into an uncomfortable personal experience, I am often met with resistance and judgment. It looks like judgment of my choices, the advice that I should get therapy, or criticism of where I am in processing the experience. What I feel most is that they are not allowing me to be present in the challenging experience. Watching me flounder and being uncomfortable as I work through my challenges makes some folks so deeply uncomfortable that they need to blame me for it.

I understand that most of us experience the world by projecting our own experiences onto other people. If you don't, brilliant. But I have witnessed myself doing this many times in my life, and before I was conscious of it, I did it all the time.

The conversation led to our observations of how we know when we are allowing others to be vulnerable. Our conclusion was that when we are in a calm head space, we are able be curious and ask questions about how they feel instead of laying on the advice. We can give advice when they accept our offer of it, or when they ask us for our thoughts. I have been working hard on in my own life to not be so quick to offer advice. I aspire to have clarity when asking questions and to lead with curiosity.

The next part of our conversation flowed into a two part question of 1) when are we allowing someone the room to be vulnerable and explore themselves (while we are able to listen and be supportive), and 2) when are we allowing someone to behave in a way that is indulging in poor behavior or thoughts (and we then become their accomplish in negative behavior)?

This question feels like a Pandora's Box because this is not an exact science and we can easily misstep in the process.

What I know is that vulnerability needs to be built with trust and over time. For any of us to feel safe in being vulnerable, we must have had the experience of being supported when sharing personal experiences. Over time, most of us are able to understand whether or not someone is trustworthy. One way we experience mistrust is when someone is judgmental towards us and our experiences: judgment erodes trust.

An answer to part one of the question would be that in order to allow others to be able to feel vulnerable with us, we have to have the discipline to show up 'big' for ourselves. Being big means we choose not reach out to someone when we know they are not good for us. It also means that before we are able to allow someone else to be vulnerable we have to be patient, loving and kind with ourselves. Being kind and loving takes work. We can't force ourselves to be loving and kind; it takes practice and effort. We need to make a contract with ourselves to be soft instead of forcing ourselves to perform.

Part two of the question, and where the practice gets tricky, is that it is important to allow people to process and move through the big things in their lives. We have to learn to hold space for others to be themselves and have their own experiences. We need to support them by being curious rather than imposing our judgement.

However, when we have witnessed someone go through the same story (or a similar story) over and over again, when is it time to step in and offer our insights or call them out on a pattern that is not supporting their growth? There is no exact science to this. One solution is to ask if they want to hear what we have to say. Being kind with our words is the important part. We can offer that we have witnessed this happen multiple times, but without being judgmental or critical. Here is the trick: if it doesn't land for them and they leave feeling unsupported, the only recourse is to apologize and ask how you could do better next time. Maybe it is that the topic is 'off-limits' for advice, and all they really need is someone who can listen. If it becomes tiring to hear it repeated, you could simply make an agreement to not speak about that specific topic.

Regardless, it is important to support our friends and family. As precarious that line can be, it takes trial and error. When we have a misstep we must learn to own it and offer our sincerest apologies.

May we all learn to be brave enough to allow ourselves and others to be vulnerable and have honest heartfelt conversations with ourselves and others.

# 10

## You Are Amazing

If someone asked me to describe you in
just 2 words, I'd say...simply amazing.
Unknown

Y ou are absolutely spectacular; you have a light
within you that sparkles. You may not have seen
it recently, but trust me, it's there. You are beautiful
inside and out. You have talents no one else has. You
have life experiences that no one else has. You are fun
to be around.

Did you know that **belief creates reality**? What do
you believe about yourself? How many times a day do
you compare yourself to others? What do you think

when you wake up and look at yourself in the mirror? Do you have nice things to say to yourself? Do you give yourself compliments? How many times a day do you allow thoughts of unworthiness to stroll around in your mind without consequence?

If you're anything like me, that may happen endlessly every day. Some days I wake up in the morning, look in the mirror and tell myself how awful I look. That I am not worthy of my dreams. Some days I even believe I am not worthy of my friends! But you know what I do on those mornings? When I watch myself walking down the critical road of *I am not awesome today*?

On attentive days, I stop myself in my thoughts. I remind myself that those thoughts are just that, thoughts, and I can choose differently. I can choose thoughts that serve my heart, my dreams and most importantly, my deep inner love for myself.

If you don't know Brené Brown, she is worthy of checking out. If you are familiar with her work then you know she is an amazing researcher and storyteller. Brené Brown has done extensive research on worthiness, and she says the only difference between people who have a strong sense of love and belonging, and those who do not, is **worthiness**. Meaning that those who feel that they are **worthy** have a **strong sense of love and belonging**.

"The one thing that keeps us out of connection with others is our fear that we are not worthy of connection." Brené Brown.

Let me tell you today, you are worthy. You are worthy of seeing how amazing you are. You are worthy of feeling good. You are worthy of your dreams. You have a light within you that is worthy of sharing. You have purpose, even if you do not yet feel it. We need your light on this planet.

If you struggle with feeling your amazing-ness I have a **change your life tip** for you today.

Grab a pen and paper.

Write down **as many amazing things that you can think of** about yourself; don't hesitate for a second. **Anything,** big or small. Such as, "I'm a great cook", "I am generous", "I am a talented painter", "I am kind", "I have a big heart", "I'll try anything once", "I am a great parent", or "I am a good friend". You know what you are.

Now, every morning when you wake up, take a deep hard look at that list. Then brush your teeth and carry on with your day. That's it. Do that every morning for the next month (or at least the next week).

Watch what happens when you start your day with worthy thoughts about yourself.

Keep notes on how it feels to wake up knowing **you are amazing**. Pay attention to what happens in your life. What happens when you begin to understand that your beliefs shape your reality?

I'd love to hear your stories, so share if you like.

You Are Amazing

# 11

## Transformation Takes Time

Nothing happens until the **pain** of remaining
the same **outweighs** the pain of change.
Arthur Burt

If you are on a spiritual path, or a path of self-
evolution, thank you. Thank you for showing up in
your life. Thank you for doing the work, even when it's
difficult. Thank you for being curious and for choosing
to be an explorer of your inner mapping. It is the
greatest work that we can do in this world because
if we can learn to show up for ourselves, to unpack
the shame, sadness and emotions that sometimes
overwhelm us, we are more capable of making dramatic
shifts and changes in our world.

It is easy to get lost in the realm of comparison even when we are learning to be kinder to, and more aware of, ourselves. Sometimes it can feel like we 'should' know better or be able to 'do' better. When we look at our personal process in that way, we are being unkind and impatient.

When I started this practice of learning to be 'conscious', I was in my early 20s and my wounds were so great. I felt like all I was doing was licking them; I was ready to pounce on anyone that breathed too intensely near my open sores.

This process has been a long one for me; I am still in it, and will be forevermore as I practice being conscious in my life. At the beginning, I was impatient and critical of myself. In retrospect, the more critical I became of myself for not 'knowing better', the harder I was on those around me. I am embarrassed to admit that I was fierce in my judgement of others. I have now learned that if I own my struggles, I am less ravaged by shame. My definition of consciousness is 'to be aware of how we respond to the world, and to have the ability to see when we are triggered and to learn to love ourselves instead of reacting to the outside world".

Change, or the process of transformation, is available to all of us. At any moment in our lives, no matter our age, we can choose to shift and evolve. We don't have to remain in the same patterns for the rest of our lives. When the same situations seem to be on repeat – when we continue to attract the same kind of undesired people in our lives, or we are stuck in a certain feeling – we can choose to wake up to the fact that something isn't working for us. Then we can start the slow climb up to change.

I have learned, now that I am (happily) older, that transformation doesn't happen overnight. It is a slow motion evolution. It comes in slow digestible moments, and it takes us time to review and decide how we feel. We learn what feelings we want to create more of in our lives, and we find ways to step away from the things we no longer want. We literally change the structure of our bodies as we begin to respond differently and feel differently. The shifts in our cellular body transform the way we are in the world.

I think the best way to move through beliefs and patterns is to have an accountability partner. Someone you can make a commitment with, someone to whom you can reach out and say, "I am struggling" or "I need help" or "I had a personal win today!". It needs to be a mutual relationship with someone who can share the same things with you (this can't be a one-sided thing). The practice is to create space for each other to fumble and fail; it is to find someone you can hold when they need to be held and someone who can hold you in return.

A dear friend and I have established some very specific language with each other to help us navigate our feelings and find ease in our communication. She came up with it: she would used the word 'turtling' when she was feeling shame and wanted to hide. Recently, when I was with her, I came across someone who triggered me emotionally. All I had to say was, "I'm turtling, I'm turtling". It was an S.O.S that meant, "Please don't make me explain, just support me as I move through this event". She knew what I meant and was right by my side supporting me until I got my bearings back. She didn't try to justify or to change me, she just witnessed my stress and allowed me to be me in it. She has been a huge gift in my life and so has this language that allows us to explain ourselves without having to have wisdom in our language for what we are feeling. As we unpacked it, we also came up with the image of a scorpion when we wanted to lash out from our pain. She once asked me how my heart was doing, after a particularly vulnerable time with another human, and I said, "My heart is 'scorpioning". It was simple and clear and, when we connected later, she could ask me specific questions about what that meant.

We need people to support us on our paths, and we are always a path. I am far from figuring it all out. It's just that now I am just less caught up in my shameful feelings because I can admit what I am going through. I am no longer responding to the circumstances of my days with an undertone of shame and embarrassment. I am moving with an open heart because I feel supported in being me with those around me and, most importantly, with myself. I am much sweeter and gentler with my world than I have ever been.

Do you have support? Do you feel loved for who you are? If not, please don't think you are failing because you don't have those things in your life. Use this as a guidepost and build that support into your beautiful life.

We are transforming as long as we are here in this human form, and as long as we are willing participate in our lives.

# 12

# What Does Acting BIG Really Mean?

You are what you think. So just think
big, believe big, act big, work big, give big,
forgive big, love big, laugh big and live big.
Andrew Camegie

*Listen:* we **all** set ourselves up with limitations. We set ourselves in relationships (friendships and otherwise) that help us sustain our beliefs of ourselves. We do it because it is easy to remain in those places. It takes great courage to accept that we are worth more than we currently believe.

Here's something to ponder: **our beliefs create our life**. What you believe, what you devote your thoughts to, **creates your reality**. Without a doubt. There is no one else creating your life for you.

Are you a person that always talks about the weather, as if it's constantly trying to undermine your happiness? Is the rain, the snow or the clouds in control of how you feel today? When someone asks how you're doing, do you say OK and then list off all the things you find frustrating about the people or circumstances around you?

If you're undermining your **bigness** by playing into the endless unconscious rants in your mind, or by surrounding yourself with people who want to keep you small, it's understandable. We all do it. The good news is that now that you are aware of your tendencies it's time to pay attention.

To implement the changes that can bring you higher takes a willingness to embrace both your capacity to achieve and your right to access your own greatness. You have to believe that you were born to reach your fullest potential in this lifetime.

Begin to notice your thoughts and ask if each particular thought serves you. If you recognize that it doesn't, choose a different one. It's a simple practice, but one that takes a lifetime to master so be patient with yourself. Start to build the muscles in your mind that support greater awareness and mindful actions.

# 13

## Here Is What I've Learned

You have to keep breaking your
heart, until it opens.
Rumi

It took a low moment in my life to realize how deep
my fear of honesty was, and how it stopped me
from saying the most important things to the most
important people in my life.

This past summer, my mother passed away. She was
a loving mother, who devoted her life to motherhood.
She was a single mother of three girls (we were six,
four and two years old when my parents separated).
Everything she did was to support us. She gave up her

dreams for us. I think because she had given up so much, by the time she could come up for air she didn't even realize what her dreams were anymore.

She made a few poor choices in life, which lead to an unhealthy lifestyle. In the end, those choices contributed to her passing.

The day she passed was difficult, but I was there to say goodbye. But I held back so much of what I wanted to say. I couldn't find the courage to say what I wanted to that day or in the weeks leading up to that day.

I don't have regrets, I have lessons. The lesson in this is how I choose to process deep loss in my life: I have learned to make peace with my choices and focus on how I can move forward with greater wisdom.

Here is what I learned from this experience: *Leave nothing worth saying unsaid.* I have lost both my mother and father now. I left a lot unsaid. I was afraid to say what I was feeling because I was afraid to get emotional. I was afraid that my emotions would devastate them, and maybe me.

Because I was afraid, I didn't tell them how deeply I love them, how important they were in my life or how I grateful I am for the choices they made. Their choices challenged my life and made me the person I am today.

My fear held me back.

I am at peace with both experiences, because I know that they can hear me today. They know how much I love them.

But as I move forward, I challenge myself to be honest and to tell the people around me the things that matter most. I am not perfect at it, I am maybe not even great at it. But I am a work in progress. That progress reminds to me leave nothing worth saying unsaid.

We are all practicing humans, and none of us is perfect. But in your practice (of being human) today, what have you left unsaid? Is there someone in your life that is unaware of how important they are to you? We can assume people know, but the truth is, unless we speak it, they have no idea.

I encourage you to take the risk. You have no idea how you may impact a loved one's life in the most loving way today.

Take risks, and trust me: it will be worth it in the end.

# 14

# Make Space for New Thoughts

If you realized how powerful your thoughts are
you'd never think a negative thought again.
Unknown

Are you swallowed by thoughts that feel gritty and
unpleasant at times? Does your mind feel like a
train out of control – racing down a track that never
seems to end? Do you wonder if you're the only one
who feels or thinks this way?

You're not alone. So many of us get trampled by our
thoughts. We feel alone in the space of ourselves.

Do you wonder how you can flip the switch on those
thoughts?

Let me ease some of your pain. It's normal. It is part of being human. Being human means we have to work to create peace in our minds and bodies. In order to do that, we have to learn to create spaces between our thoughts.

How do you do that when you're in a train of thought that seems to be travelling down a track that doesn't end?

Take a moment to step back and take a breath. Focus on your breath for a moment, or five moments.

Have you ever heard the phrase, 'What you think creates your reality'?

It is one hundred percent true. What we think creates our reality and our lives. No one else can create those for us. We can change our thoughts at any given moment and thus change our reality.

My question for you is "What would you **rather** be thinking?".

If you want to create a different reality in your life, the first thing you need to do is learn to get quiet and create space for breath. It's rather simple. The next time you're watching yourself getting attached to a reaction in your mind – something that screams or whispers "This is who I am" – stop and breathe. Breathe enough to calm the reactive place in your body.

The next step is to choose a different thought. **Yes,** it's that simple! But it requires a tremendous amount of inner strength to trust in yourself enough to choose a different thought. Choose to stick with the new thought for as many breaths as you can in order to let the old thought go.

Creating change in thought patterns and in your life requires a commitment to becoming a conscious human. It takes work, like building any new skill. It takes work to run five kilometers or a marathon. It takes work to learn how to ride a bike or swim, to learn algebra or a new language. However, many of us learned these skills when we were young, and we forget that as we age we still need to build skills, to cultivate an inner environment of endless learning and growth.

Are you willing to put work into yourself? No matter the stage of your life?

If you are, watch your world change around you. Trust me. It's worth paying attention and witnessing the awesomeness of peace in your mind and body.

I have faith in your capacity to thrive in your inner work. The question is, do you?

# 15

# Be Responsible for Your Energy

Take responsibility for the energy you bring.
Dr. Jill Bolte Taylor

You know when you run into someone – on the street, in the grocery store or at a party – and within minutes of chatting with them, you feel drained? You can feel like it's hard to hold on to the place within you that felt good before connecting with them. I use the term 'energy vampire' for these folks because that is essentially what you are experiencing: they are sucking the energy right out of you.

Listen, we all have challenging days and events in our life. We **all** have days where we feel drained and need to articulate some of our frustrations to our friends. But the question is: do you do it **all** the time?

We can indulge in our stories in a way that they become an energy drain on ourselves and others. I like to think of it like this: When I am struggling with a challenge, I need to talk about it with one or two people, but when I start to share with more people it becomes a story or drama that takes over my experience.

I like to remember that even when I am out and about, my thoughts have tremendous weight and are very powerful. If I am regularly walking around feeling grumpy or having unhappy thoughts about myself (or others), it **will** affect those around me. You know that feeling when you walk by someone you don't even know on the street and they feel dark? That's what I'm talking about.

We need to be responsible for what we are feeding our minds because that has a direct effect on our bodies and on those around us.

We are living in tumultuous times. Socially, globally and politically. It matters how we deliver ourselves to the world and how we contribute to it. It matters who you are when you are at home, at work, at the grocery store or in your car.

I am not suggesting you walk around with forced or fake positivity. I am suggesting that you really pay attention to how you are offering yourself to your community, and that you understand how you feel affects those around you. This is not meant to scare you if you are dealing with challenges, or if you have deep, dark fears, but if that is the case I would encourage you to seek help. Do your personal work so you can become an agent of change that our world so desperately needs.

The world needs **your** light.

# 16
## Stop Playing Small

Your playing small does not serve the world.
Marianne Williamson

I know, it's bold to tell you to **stop**. I mean you no disrespect, I am simply reminding you to witness your inner voice.

This is so important. I believe that if you can **stop playing small,** your whole life will change.

Do you see your potential? Do you understand you are more than what your thoughts tell you?

I want you to know that you are an amazing person, with a bright, beautiful heart.

You are perfect just as you are. Who you are in this moment can choose to stop playing small.

What I am saying is that your brilliance is beckoning to come out, *you are unique*, and there is no other person in the world with your specific set of talents and skills and life experience.

It's time to stop comparing yourself to others. Stop listening to the voice within that wants to debunk your dreams. Are you putting aside your desires because you believe you are making the best decisions for everyone else in your life?

What if you understood that once you start making decisions based on what is best for **your** life, the true identity of your heart shines.

You are worthy of your dreams, no matter how small or large they are. We live in a tremendous time on this planet, and we can make our dreams our realities.

Here is my question for you today – in what ways are you playing small? What are your dreams? Are you choosing to pay attention to them?

Or perhaps **you are** paying attention and following your dreams already. If so, that is so very awesome.

Be present and tune into your breath today friend, it will change your life.

# 17

# Can You Be Comfortable with Being Disliked?

You will never be criticized by someone who
is doing more than you. You will only be
criticized by someone doing less.

Our desire to be liked can be linked with not living
for ourselves. It is a symptom of choosing to live
based on the judgements of others instead of living our
own authentic lives.

I have learned that those who learn to make choices
for themselves, and find the courage to move beyond
the judgement of others can make a big impact in their
own lives and in the lives of others. There is a level of

resiliency that they have developed, that helps them remember their own thoughts are way more valuable than the criticism of others. It is a sort of tenacity, a strength that is built from within.

I had the amazing opportunity to hear Barack Obama speak live not long before writing this book: What made this even more extraordinary was that almost exactly a year before, I had also heard Michelle Obama speak. During her talk, I had sat third row centre; she was essentially right in front of me. Both experiences were exceptional. The wave of energy I felt when each of them walked on stage was like nothing I have ever felt before. I experienced a cocktail of admiration, awe, respect and disbelief as I found myself sitting near two people I greatly appreciate. I was so overcome with emotion that my tears spoke for me.

The reason I respect them, individually and as a couple, is because they both came from nothing. They built lives based on unimaginable opportunities solely because – at the core – they had visions for a better world and they believed they could help create it. Underscored by an unwavering commitment to share from a place of love, their missions led them to step into (arguably) the most powerful and impactful roles on the globe. They could only achieve this because they believed in their vision wholeheartedly that they were able to risk not being liked and chose to be unwaveringly vulnerable. Their mission ended up exposing many aspects of their lives and beliefs on the world stage.

Most of us are not risking our lives (or our children's lives) if we follow our dreams and find the courage to follow our dreams. With that understanding, what is holding you back from having a voice and living your life for **you**? Whose judgment scares you?

Professionally, I run a business, teach yoga, life coach, facilitate retreats and trainings and publish a weekly blog while dabbling in motivational speaking. I often find myself standing in front of people speaking my truth and living a life different than any example I was given growing up.

I speak openly with the teachers at my studio about how challenging it is for us, as teachers, to find our voices. I discuss having the ability to teach without reciting other people's words. I encourage us all to find the courage to speak our own words, to voice our truths and offer insights and teachings that move beyond scripture and come from deep within. To not react to the eye roles, yawns or disinterested looks. It takes strength from within to establish energetic boundaries. When we see someone's disinterest we must choose to stay on course instead of shifting our plan to make that one person feel better.

The reason I am so inspired by the Obamas is because they have had the courage to believe in their capacities to be agents of change. They have used the privilege of being human and found opportunities to be of service in the world. They have put themselves (over and over) in position to be judged, ridiculed and put down for their ideas and decisions. This is brave beyond what I yet know in myself.

I am an advocate for creating inner change and finding ways to be more kind, compassionate, empathetic, vulnerable and brave. I believe that by showing up and doing our inner work we can strengthen our missions in this world. I am a proponent for this. At the foundation of my mission is the opportunity to strengthen my love for myself so I am able to spread kindness through my work.

So here are the questions: What is your passion? What lights up your heart? How do you want to make the people around you feel? Understanding these concepts will help you with your mission; they will be the north stars to guide you toward your goals in life. They will help eradicate the doubt and judgement you hear from others. They will allow you to follow your heart and cease caring about what someone else might think of you. They will give you the courage to start your own business, to ask someone out, to volunteer for an organization that calls to you, to open your heart without fear of being hurt, to support someone who needs help, to be honest about your sexual orientation or to offer an idea that is against popular opinion.

Who is someone that you admire? Find ways to channel their courage by stepping up in your own life and owning your desires. Choose to live a life that is authentic to you by being courageous enough to be you. That is it. Don't listen to anyone who tells you that you are not worthy of being you. You will never be criticized by someone who is doing more than you. You will only be criticized by those who are doing less.

Go on: be you, all of you, and grab your backpack full of courage.

# 18

## What's Your Measure of Success?

Success isn't about the end results, it's
about what you learn along the way.
Vera Wang

What is your measure of success? Seriously?
Before you read on, think about it. What do you
believe success looks like in your life?

I used to believe success looked like this: power suits,
money, custom built houses and cars, comparison
and competition, luxury vacations and a life spent
working away.

This has completely changed over the years. Today, I
believe my relationship with a much different version of

success has created more balance and sustainability in my life. I believe my current views fill the hollow places in my heart that I had created with my fictitious ideas of success.

Today I work very hard at not comparing myself to others, and I constantly remind myself what my success looks like now.

Only we can define our own success. No one else has the capacity to measure our success. If someone else tries, it's time to evaluate what purpose they have within your inner workings. Why are they so committed to your success? Better yet, why do you care?

I'll share with you what my success looks like, not as a measure to compare against, but as an example of how you can look inside yourself to find your own unique version of success.

To me, success is equal to feeling whole and open to pleasure. It is feeling that I have more space for breath than for stress and feeling like I have time to connect to my heart without judgement. Success is knowing that I am moved by **love** and not by my **fears**.

I know my life is abundant when I have quality time with my daughter, and when I give her time to connect to me in the ways that serve her (not me). Being present for my daughter when she needs me is a huge measure of success for me. Another way I measure success is when I get exercise on a regular and consistent basis. When I make space for loving greatly and when I have time to give to others. When I have a quality roof over my head and beautiful place to lie my head. When I can afford to feed myself and loved ones healthy food. When I have time to connect with friends. When I practice gratitude every day.

When I look at creating success, I need to look at what I want to create in my life. I am building toward having more income for my retirement and dream accounts and for the amount of money I use for my humanitarian causes. I want to travel more and teach my daughter to experience the world with humility so we can find ways to be agents of change together in this world.

What have your measurements of success been up until now? Are they still serving you? Do the standards you set in the past still resonate with you? Are you ready to look at different ways to feel in your life? Does your life feel unbalanced? Are you stressed beyond being able to manage? If you want to change anything in your life, look at what you believe accomplishment looks like in your life.

If you live your success with a whole heart, your impact on your loved ones will become immeasurable.

# 19

# Cultivating Faith and Trust in Your Life

Faith is not belief without proof,
but trust without reservation.
D. Elton Trueblood

To me, faith is the unwavering conviction that something greater (the universe, God, the divine etc) is supporting us. It is trusting in the things you can't explain but know to be true in your heart.

That's what I would describe the depth of work it takes to shift your life in its entirety.

How do you rebuild your faith when you're unsure whether you can trust someone (or anyone)? How do you rebuild your faith when you have been disappointed time and time again, or when your heart has been broken?

To trust is to let go, to let go of the need to control, the need to know the outcome and have all the answers. To trust is to understand that setting goals and having dreams is of the utmost importance. When you dream and set your goals, you must then trust in the process. Revel in the journey. I don't mean you just sit back and wait for the world to unfold for you; I mean you stand up and walk toward what you want, and you take the steps to become an agent of your own creation.

When you trust, you invite positive outcomes. You welcome new experiences and new people into your life. You learn to enjoy not knowing, because you understand that you are meant to have whatever comes.

In order to trust, you must first trust yourself. Learn to be there for yourself, to say **no** when you know that is the right answer, and to say **yes** even when it scares you. When you can truly listen to your inner guidance, you have no reason to be fearful because it won't lead you astray. If you have never done this, it will take time to identify the difference between your inner ego/saboteur and your heart, or your true self.

These are teachable practices and ones you can learn by reading some of the amazing material that is available, by researching or travelling or through more structured educational opportunities. These practices are the foundation of my 50-hour *Create The Life You Want* course.

Start by being clear with where you are feeling distrust, and notice any way you are unable to listen to your inner guidance system.

Then use your abilities to be patient but clear, to be kind and direct, and to set boundaries that are guided by understanding instead of defiance. Create a passion for learning to trust in the things you don't understand. Most importantly, stop trying to control and instead sit with the sweet surrender of trust. Once you begin to trust and to have faith in the unknown, you will see the magic that is created in your life when you have faith.

## 20
## Can We All Just Stop Being So Good?

Be careful who you pretend to be.
You may forget who you are.
Unknown

Here I go, on my soapbox: for goodness' sake, can we all just stop being so darn **good?** You know, when someone asks you, "How are you?" and without missing a beat your automatic response is "good"? You know there is no quality to it. Even as the word slips out of your mouth, you probably know there is a more authentic answer to that question. How on Earth are you going to be able to speak your truth in this world if you can't even answer that simple question honestly?

I get it, I really do. I answer, "I'm good!" because I don't want to be too honest for fear of being judged or taking up too much of someone's time. Sometimes I worry that someone might not want to speak to me again because I'm too much, or too real.

Can you imagine if we all just spoke our truths? We would be able to say, "Actually, I'm shitty", or "I just got in an argument, and I feel raw", or "I am too tired/hungry/bored/sad/distracted/ to talk"? When we gloss over our answers, we give other people permission to do the same. We don't encourage real exchange. When you answer, "I am good" no one says, "Really? Tell me all the ways you are good. Give me an actual glimpse of your current experience". An expected answer excuses you from sharing too much about yourself. You don't have to explain **why** you're good. You also don't have the opportunity to share all the ways you are fantastically happy or proud of yourself or in love.

Instead, the next time someone asks, you could just sweetly and honestly be gloriously honest and move on. Bam! Just like that.

When you do this, when you are beautifully honest, you'll be able to move through conversation with more of your true self, with a bit less of the veil of protection that holds you back from just being you. Sweet ol' you.

Try it today. For the entire day, be honest about how you are doing. Check in with yourself every time you have the opportunity to answer the question and see how it feels to be unapologetically honest. Did you find a bit of yourself in there, buried under layers of self-protective habits or assumptions about others' interests in you? When you give it a chance to speak, that quiet place in you takes a big-assed exhale because it feels so darn good to be exposed.

You'll undoubtedly have to practice not worrying about how anyone else responds to your honesty. It may make some people uncomfortable. It may raise some eyebrows. As a society, we are very comfortable with being "good!", and it's a habit that won't be broken overnight. But isn't finding your truth worth a little discomfort?

An honorable mention in this practice is the skill of being a **good listener.** This is separate topic but touching on it has value. It's good to ask someone how they are as though you mean it (because hopefully you do), and **not** to ask if you don't have the time or energy to hold space and attention for their answer. Authentic conversation is ultimately a two-way street.

# 21

# Are You Discerning in Your Friendships?

Real love doesn't meet you at your
best. It meets you at your mess.
J.S Park

Friendships fill us up. Our connection to other humans sustains our well-being. Friendship is knowing you have someone to lean on when you need it. It's the feeling that you can connect with someone in the dark as well as the joyful times of life. We thrive on connecting with others: it's what keeps us alive. Without it we can become deeply lonely, cynical, thirsty for touch and really sad.

There are many ways we can create connection in our lives whether through work, recreation, social gatherings, intimate relationships, friends or family. I want to find my go-to, been-in-the-trenches-with-you soul sisters or brothers that I can hold close in the good and bad times.

Sometimes, however, we make poor choices and trust the wrong people. I have. Like many of us, I have found the courage to divulge my deep, dark secrets. Sharing them is a deeply vulnerable act and it can be destructive if they are not respected. I have mistakenly trusted the wrong people with my secrets and been so poorly treated that I, as a result, became completely disoriented in **all** of my relationships. In the past, if I trusted someone with details about myself (someone with whom I thought I was sharing a sacred and trusting relationship), and they hurt me, I would have decided I couldn't trust myself to choose wisely.

Here is what I now know: I know that friendships are built. I know that friendships develop over time. I know that the friends who are willing to see you for all that you are, in your hardest struggles, with your deepest secrets, the ones who will celebrate with you when you finally find success, are limited to one, maybe two, and if you're really lucky, three in a lifetime. It takes time to find out if someone is going to stick around. I am discerning early on in my relationships so that I can weave through some of the muddy communication and avoid wasting time on the wrong connections.

In Dr. Brené Brown's research on belonging, she discovers that true friendships and connections come when they are "not at the cost of your authenticity, freedom and power". This is a fantastic measure to check in with. Do you have to make sacrifices to your authenticity, freedom or power in order to hold a relationship? If so, it is absolutely worth evaluating that relationship.

Have you ever been so completely loved by someone that when you called them in a somber, snot-running, tear-streaming state, they said, "I'm coming, I'm here for you"? Someone who did not try to talk you out of feeling what you were feeling, but was there hold your hand when 'sadness' was too plain a word to explain how you felt?

It's so easy to be friends with people when they are happily enjoying life and thriving in any endeavor. No problem. It's when we are challenged that we know who our friends are. Truly.

What kind of friend are you? Are you able to be there for your close friends, are you able to listen without needing to express your opinions? Are you able to work on those friendships and not turn away when you see something you don't like? Are you able to go to that soul sister or brother in the biggest devastation of their lives, know that their story is theirs and not yours, and sit with them in their pain without being overcome by it? Can you take their hand, sit patiently and say, "I am here"?

What kind of friendships do you want more of? What is most important to you? Have you ever considered that before? You get to choose who surrounds you. You have permission to give more to those who are dear to your heart and spend far less time with those who drain you.

Dr. Brené Brown also states that you can "learn to be present with people without having to sacrifice who you are".

Be discerning with yourself and with whom you let into your inner sanctum. Once someone is in my inner circle I will honor and respect them. I protect those I love (including myself) with a intense fierceness. I will do anything for them. I will support and encourage them. I will let them **be** as long as I receive the same in return. I will love with all my heart.

In what ways are you discerning?

## 22

# Wisdom Is Built, Not Bestowed

Those who look outside, dreams.
Those who look inside, awakes.
Carl Jung

Wisdom. Isn't wisdom a beautiful word? I find it so lovely. So clear and kind, so graceful and intelligent. When used with intention, words can be so powerful; when used without thought, they can be destructive.

I heard Danielle Laporte speak of wisdom in an interview. She said, "Wisdom is built, not bestowed". I have understood that concept for a long time, but I **love** the way she worded it.

You are not gifted with something at birth that makes you wiser. You aren't granted wisdom because of who your parents are or the color of your skin or where you were born. Wisdom is earned. It is gathered from hardship. It is cultivated through really hard life lessons, the awful times that bring us to our knees when we find ourselves praying for our own salvation and don't know if we will make it through. Wisdom can be found there. It is in heartache, in the loss of our loved ones, in desperate financial times, in the gaping unknown of our futures. It is in understanding that we don't have to have all the answers and in being open to being humbled by our own actions.

Wisdom is the difference between blaming others for your experiences and owning your own life. When you own your reality you understand that you are the creator of your story. No one else. You are the one who decides how you will learn your lessons. When you wake up to your struggles, you are the one who decides. You can decide to use your wisdom to help you with any challenge. Wisdom is what picks you up by the shirt and says, "You've got this". Wisdom reminds us to keep our judgments to ourselves, or better yet, to turn our judgments into compassion and kindness.

Your life is filled with opportunities to grow and become gentler with yourself and others. Life is digested rather than consumed. Hard times ask us to look inside and slow down. Take deep breaths. Remember: you are not alone, even though you may be alone in this moment and in this story.

Life is a gift filled with opportunities to grow your wisdom. Are you celebrating this? Are you holding your wisdom close and swimming in gratitude for all of the things you get to learn and all the ways you can be of service to others? Or are you looking at all of your opportunities as crappy offerings from the universe?

Choose your perspective wisely.

# 23
# Tread Lighter in Challenging Times

Difficult roads often lead to
beautiful destinations.
Unknown

There are tumultuous times in the world right now.
For a lot of people. Including me.

It also seems like people have amplified anger and
frustration with everything that is happening around
them. There are so many ways in which we are
witnessing acts of hatred and fear, like the devastation
we experience with gun violence.

There is an automatic quality to the anger and hatred
that is taking hold, and this worries me. I see it

demonstrated in our homes and in our workplaces. I see it on social media and in the news in ways I have never seen in my lifetime. We have never before had the capacity to share our unedited thoughts so **immediately**. So swiftly.

There is also an eagerness to our responses, a participation in reaction rather than an effort to take the time to slow down and think about how to respond. When we slow down, we get to choose the outcomes we desire. We have the opportunity to create space and find gentleness in our words and actions. We have time to take deep breaths. Most importantly, we can learn to not say everything that comes to our minds. We can take time to consider what we **want** to say and recognize that our words and ideas are what we offer of ourselves to the world. Words are more powerful than we give them credit for. Words have a power that moves our lives, and our degree of consciousness about how we use them affects our experiences deeply.

Today, I continue to work on having softer responses. This doesn't mean that I am less affected by what occurs around and to me; it means I choose how I engage with my life. First, I pay attention to how I am triggered by others' words and actions and I observe the raw emotions and the impulses to blindly react as they rise within me. Then I step back and ask myself if that is really me. Do I really need to respond with such aggression and haste?

I am not perfect, and I make mistakes. But when I take the time to think about what I want to see in my immediate world, which is **a deeper and more**

**vulnerable love,** I slow down. Because love is built. It is a choice. Love is not blind ignorance. Love is moving beyond ignorance. I am learning to make choices to respond from **love** instead of from fear and hate.

When I choose that kinder, discerning place from which to speak, I respond from love for myself and my family and friends. It is a love that softens and is inclusive. It is a love that is generous even when it feels like I would have more control if I could limit the amount of love I dole out. I seek to move from the part of me that is not selective about who receives my love. This kind of attention takes work. To choose to respond toward rather than fight means I have to see my reactive tendencies and overcome them, all before I say a single word.

It is a practice, because it is not easy. Practice takes work and is continuous. But the alternative is choosing to live in a world that is reactive and unkind; one that perpetuates the darkness that some people and circumstances deliver to our world. Practicing being kind is not easy work. Easy work means burying our heads in the sand, blaming others for our experience or projecting our experience onto others. If you want to challenge yourself, think about the world you want to create and begin to understand that you can do this by thoughtfully shaping your response to the world.

You'll become a leader in your family, workplace as well as within your community by choosing to tread more lightly in challenging times.

## 24
## Boundaries

Clear is kind, unclear is unkind.
Dr. Brené Brown

When I learned to set boundaries, I began to change my world. I was able to release some of the dramas that were littering my life. Since then, I have had interesting conversations around the word 'boundaries' and found that some folks do not understand what it means. Some also do not know how to set boundaries. A few years ago, I had a friend who believed the word boundaries was offensive and hard. This was challenging because we were doing business together and a large portion of the problems we were experiencing was because of the weakness in our boundaries. People were not treating us how we'd hoped they would because we were not setting proper boundaries.

When we have weak boundaries people may walk all over us. We feel disconnected from ourselves and taken advantage of; we feel shame for making choices that don't feel good. We might even isolate ourselves from others and avoid conflict because we are struggling to have clarity in our own beliefs.

There is phrase I've recently picked up from Brené Brown: "Clear is kind, unclear is unkind". I find this summarizes the need for an honest relationship with ourselves. We can only set boundaries when we are clear with ourselves and when we know how we want to be treated as well as how we want to treat other people. This means we must learn to be honest with ourselves, something a lot of us are not very skilled at.

In my business – when I first started almost a decade ago – I had a weak sense of self. I had confidence in my business skills, but I the over-arching program playing in my mind was that I was not good enough. I was so worried about being liked and doing the 'right' thing that I was ravished by feelings of being an imposter. I had poor boundaries with myself (because I wanted to make everyone happy) and so others were constantly taking advantage of me. This was happening simply because I didn't believe I was worthy of respect. I was so busy with a new baby and a business that I became addicted to the sensation of being busy and unconsciously used it is as excuse to avoid being clear with myself and others.

Once I identified that I had a poor relationship with myself and how that was constantly creating drama in my life, I began a radical transformation of connecting with what it was that I truly wanted. When I was able to identify that I was not having honest conversations because I was allowing the belief of 'I am not good enough' to run my life, my life started to radically change.

Boundaries are about deciding how you want to be treated and, in turn, how you want to treat other people. Ultimately, I believe if we are setting boundaries from a place that lacks self-awareness and gentleness we will eventually be met with some kind of struggle. With lack of honest conversation with ourselves we will blame others for experiences that happen around us – otherwise known as projecting our inner world onto others. When we are not showing respect for ourselves if we are constantly changing our plans/ minds to please others instead of doing the things we actually want to do. Our friends will not hold up our boundaries if, in some capacity, they witness our lack of self-respect as we flail with our own boundaries.

Boundaries are about deciding how we want to feel and what we want. They show we respect ourselves enough to show up and speak our truths even when they are uncomfortable. But setting boundaries is unsettling work and it requires us to have authentic conversations with ourselves. It requires us to stop making excuses as to why we will tolerate certain things in order to feed our lack of self-worth. Where our boundaries should be becomes clear the more we are willing to show up in our own lives.

We meet all kinds of people in our lives and there are some people that it feels easy to be clear and honest with. With others, it can feel like we struggle to be heard. They may be so committed to pushing their own agenda they aren't able to hear us. It is in those moments that we need the solid practice of having genuine conversations with ourselves and being able to set steady boundaries. This practice will push us to be firm.

Where are you struggling in your life? In what ways do you feel people are walking over you? What are you not being honest with yourself about? Are you willing to start listening to what it is you really feel and want?

It is important to decide how you want to feel. But simply knowing how you want to feel doesn't necessarily help you set boundaries. To find that, you must decide if you're ready to honour how you want to feel and take the actions – which requires hard work – required to get there? Do you feel you are worth it?

I think you are.

## 25

# Can You Change in The Moment?

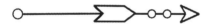

The choices we make not affect
the opportunities in the future.
Chris Guillebeau

The ability to change our minds is one of the many
wonders of being human. The ability to catch our
thoughts in the palms of our minds is more than a
gift: it is a skill that we develop by being mindful and
creating opportunities to watch our emotions ebb and
flow.

Even more astounding is our power to sustain this
practice when we are being challenged. To remain
present enough to change our responses in the very

moment we are being pushed takes so much **courage.** It's a practice of digging deep and finding space to see that choices are always there. We just have to learn to see them.

This is a practice that is transformational.

When you're in your car and someone cuts in front of you, narrowly missing you, and you choose to slam on the horn and wave your middle finger out the window, it doesn't solve anything and likely leaves you feeling empty and angry. What if you changed your mind in that moment? What if you chose to drink in a deep breath, relax, and see that this 'offender' may need some tenderness rather than being shown that they were wrong (which they likely already know). Your assault may leave them feeling even more depleted and small.

It takes courage to change your response to any given situation, to move out of the automatic response in your body. To not react when your husband, lover or partner pushes your buttons. Or to finally stand up for yourself after being silent for too long.

You already have so much courage within you. I promise. It lives deep within your cells and it knows how to come forth. Call on it. Ask for it. Ask to be shown where it hides; ask your courage to guide you. Your strength will respond to this call. It will show up. Trust me. It's the support you've been seeking outside of yourself, but you never needed to look any further than you.

Change your mind, change your career, change your reactions. Do something that has always scared you. Take that course. Have a child. Open your heart to love. Go out to the party even though you already said "no". See what magic enters your life when you learn how to change your automatic responses. We get transformational opportunities all the time and practicing daily conscious choice-making lays the foundation for the bigger moments.

Go into the world; seek out moments to change the way you respond to yourself.

# 26

## How Do You Trust Without Being Scared?

To forgive is to set a prisoner free and
to discover that prisoner was you.
Lewis B. Smedes

Trust.

Big word. Big Meaning. Big emotion behind the word.
I think trust is built. Within. It is a journey of learning
to trust yourself. To trust yourself to make the right
decisions for you. To trust that you can pick yourself
up after heartache. To trust in your ability to be there

for yourself, when you need it most, when you're at your most vulnerable and really scared.

Trust is learning that no matter what happens you will be OK, because you have the skills to deal with anything that comes your way. Trusting yourself also means that when you are falling apart, you have the ability to ask for help in ANY way you need. It doesn't mean you expect other people to be there for you all the time. It doesn't mean you can't do it on your own. But when life is throwing a challenge at you that feels unmanageable, you know you can handle it or that you can ask for help.

Trust means that when you are being pushed to your limits, when you find yourself being challenged in a large way, your quiet inner voice can offer stability. It can guide you beyond the loud ego – the ego that hijacks your ability to make sound decisions. Trust is knowing that when you need it most, when you are most rocked, you will be able to reach deep within and find some clarity in thought – the deep inner knowing that is ready to guide you toward the path of least resistance.

Trust is built. If someone ever says, "Just trust me", but you've not had the opportunity to build trust with them...you may be right not to trust them. Trust is a commodity that takes time to establish. Within our relationships we learn if someone is trustworthy. Do they follow through on their commitments? Do they live what they speak, or do they say one thing and do another? Are they kind to others? Can they show up for you when you most need it, or when you ask?

We lose trust in ourselves when we make choices that make us feel bad, or when we lack the self-discipline to navigate away from habitual poor choices. Making better choices will improve your relationship with yourself, and you will find that your self-worth amplifies. If you struggle with feeling worthy, make the shift to make choices that feel better – the kind of choices that can feel hard to make – but when you do you will find it changes how you feel.

Most of us think trust is about trusting someone else, but I have come to understand that trust is an inside journey. It is something we develop. It means we stop giving away our sense of well-being when someone breaks our trust. Because no matter what, even when we are hurting, we are capable of making choices for our highest good. Even when it's hard to make good decisions, we are able to stand tall and be what we need.

The question to ask is, "Can I trust myself to show up in the ways I need"? If the answer is no, then it is time you evaluate this, and begin to strengthen your decision-making skills. You have the capacity to listen to your inner knowing/intuition, a voice which is much quieter, but so much wiser, than the ego self.

I trust your ability to make the decisions that best serve you. As I trust my ability to do the same.

# 27

# Change Your Life by Changing How You Feel

How do you spell 'love'?
Piglet

You don't spell it. You feel it.
Pooh

How do you feel most of the time? What do you notice in your response to your day to day life that feels like a consistent companion? Do you feel overworked and exhausted every day? Do you feel inspired daily? Do you feel joyful? Do you feel dread? Do you feel like you are a slave to your life and kids?

Have you ever considered how you feel when you wake up in the morning? Has the way you feel become an unconscious state? Meaning, do you think about how you feel, or do you just feel what you're feeling and believe that is how it is supposed to be?

Have you ever wondered how to change your life?

If you want to change your life you must change how you feel. In order to create different outcomes in our lives we actually have to change our feeling states – meaning the way we feel day to day and how we unconsciously respond to our world. We can fill our minds with endless positive affirmations, but if we feel empty, lonely, financially broke, hurt or broken on the inside, no amount of positive self talk will change those experiences. The only way to change these experiences is to look at how you feel.

It is not easy to change an emotional state. I know how hard it can be to change, especially if you have been living within a certain feeling state for a long time. I am regularly checking in with the responses that I have to friends, work and finances that are clearly not the way I want to feel about those things. But I continue have emotional responses that don't feel good.

In order to manage myself, and help create ease in my life, I figured out that if I followed three key practices then I can progressively create a new feeling state. The three practices I use and continue to use are:

1) Witness the emotional state. Which means stop, take three deep breaths and pay attention to your automatic emotional response. Meaning, instead of sliding down the reactive slide, I must (there is no way around this) stop myself and decide to watch what is happening. I have found that when I am really tuned into paying attention, I can learn to slow down and stop reacting.

2) Choose a different response. An example would be that you are used to never having enough time, **always** rushing around, playing catch up on time from the moment you leave the house in the morning. However, if I take the time to watch myself and slow down the moment, I will witness that immediate urge to stress about time. I can choose to move slower and decide that I am not late. In fact, I can probably leave the house ten minutes earlier than I normally do and feel really great about arriving early. All of a sudden, I have switched out of the stressful emotional state of being late.

3) Be attentive enough to stick with it the entire day. Watch yourself. Every time I have the automatic urge to respond with stress (as my example), I choose to slow down and move my mind into a different emotional state. It could be the feeling of knowing I have plenty of time, and that I can use my time to leave earlier and enjoy driving slower, arrive earlier and move slower once I get out of my car.

These steps can be applied to any emotional state, such as arguing with your kids (feeling state of frustration), agitation with people at work (feeling state of helplessness in creating change at work), feeling stressed about meeting new people (feeling state of anxiety when in new situations), public speaking (feeling state of embarrassing yourself), working your butt off so you can be recognized at work (feeling state of incompetence) or deciding to say no instead of always saying yes (feeling state of spreading yourself too thin and not being appreciated). Do you see where I am going with this? There are endless emotional states we end up in every single day. Yet, we have the privilege to choose a different response in any given moment.

How are you going to shift how you feel today?

## 28

# Who (Not What) Do You Want to Be?

Ten years from now, make sure
you can say you that you chose
your life, you didn't settle for it.
Unknown

From the time we are little children, people start asking, "What do you want to be?". Eager ears listen and expect answers like 'firefighter, dog walker, doctor, swimmer, teacher, etc.' From an early age we get fixated on measuring success by our accomplishments rather than by who we are as people.

When were you ever asked **who** you want to be? How you want to show up in your life – for yourself and others? Do you want to be kind, respectful, generous, attentive, supportive, loving, mindful and/or non-reactive? Would you like to have the inner strength to pick yourself up after enduring unimaginable pain, and look around for rainbows instead of storm clouds? To be gentle with the suffering of others? To be non-judgmental? I heard former American vice president Joe Biden quote that his mother said, "Courage is the virtue that made all the others possible." I agree. I believe courage is a quality that allows us to decide who we want to be instead of responding out of fear or pain.

It takes courage to love passionately, to open up to someone and trust that giving your love to them won't break you if it doesn't end well. It takes courage to respond to hate with love. It takes courage to decide you will say something when you see a stranger being victimized for their gender, race or social beliefs. It takes courage to create change in your life and to make **huge** changes globally and in your community. It takes courage to listen to your own intuition instead of being persuaded by social expectations or by what others think. It takes courage to choose who you want to be.

How do you want to be defined? Who around you do you admire? What traits do they possess that you would like to own?

If we think about who we want to be, then we can stop worrying about immediately gratifying outcomes and we look at our lives as the day-to-day creation of our own legacies.

At any moment, **you** can choose to become anyone you want to be. At any point, **you** can change. You can decide to be kinder or willing to see someone else's perspective. You can be willing to demonstrate your capacity to change.

This week, challenge yourself. Answer the following four questions. Put them on your bathroom mirror, in your wallet, at your desk, or anywhere that you will receive the daily reminders.

1) What traits do you admire in others?
2) What traits do you already have that you're proud of?
3) What do you want to be known for in this lifetime?
4) What trait are you going to work on building, starting today?

Most importantly, share this with anyone in your life willing and curious enough to benefit from it.

I always love hearing from you. Feel free to share your stories.

## 29

# Allow Life to Soften, Not Harden, You

What is love? Love is the
absence of judgement.
Dalai Lama

Over the years, I've witnessed friends and family members get more settled in their beliefs and become less willing to see new perspectives and different points of view. I've watched as they choose to feed or hold on to anger rather than to forgive and let go. I've seen stories stay with people for not only years but decades, and I have seen how certain beliefs have hardened them and made it more difficult for them to break through to the softer side of reason. The more time they spend in these aggressive, defensive, self-protective and sometimes delusional energies, the harder it is for them to let go of their pain.

I've seen this pain in the faces of the hardened: faces, jaws and eyes mirroring the rigidity of an internal world of thoughts and beliefs. An inability to let go and move forward creates a physical demeanor that is visible in the body and restricts the amount of joy we are able to feel in our lives. You've seen it in others: the inability to release deep pain creates a hardened exterior, like a house with thick walls, and we can't just take an emotional jackhammer of love and break it down. It is up to the holder of the pain to choose to release.

Are you hardening?

Allowing our pain to dictate a deep need to control and hold onto worn out beliefs only causes pain for ourselves, not for those that have triggered it in us.

The hardening comes from relationships with other people and the way we choose to carry those relationships in our own emotional bodies. When our trust is broken, when we believe we should have 'known better', when we internalize the hurt that comes from not being able to protect ourselves from the pain of human experience, we create a kind of scar tissue if we are not able to move through the consequent pain with mindfulness and healthy tools.

Please stop making yourself suffer for the generous teachings that hurt, pain and suffering bring to your life. When you are hurt, learn to lean into the pain and be curious about its meaning. This is not to suggest that you should live in some unrealistic state of blind positivity, accepting that pain happens to everyone and that you should see the good in all of it. No! Feel the frustration, the anger and the hurt that come with your lessons. Own those emotions and encourage them to flow in the river of your experience. Then, when it's time, choose to navigate off the river and choose not to move from that hurt for the rest of your days.

What if you saw those who have hurt you as teachers creating an opportunity to soften you, to be kinder and more loving to yourself? Often, we harden our physical body when we experience pain. What if you used the pain to bring awareness to softening your eyes and face? What if we could transform our experiences into educations for our highest learning? What if we could shift from self-harming intolerance to majestic and radiant self-exploration? What would your life be like if you could soften and stop being so certain about all of the outcomes and all that you know? You might feel better, you might be kinder to yourself. You might set an example for everyone looking into your eyes at the softness that gives them permission to soften their own gaze.

I see the softness in your eyes. Can you?

# 30
## How I Deal with Challenges

The secret of change is to focus
all your energy, not fighting the
old, but building on the new.
Socrates

I believe that in my life, and I have been gifted with an abundance of challenges. Those who know me well know I am not exaggerating here: I've been pushed to such extremes that I have fallen to my knees and said, "Enough, please. Please, no more."

I know you have been in this place as well. You may not be in challenging times right now, but I can guarantee that you have been and will be again in the future. You can't be human and not deal with challenges, whether it's overcoming the dark voices that come from within, or the actions or decisions of others that lead you down a path you did not want.

I have sought the answers to 'Why?'...Did I make some soul agreement? Am I a bad person? Do I trust the wrong people? How could I fail myself so massively? I can get caught up trying to figure out the reasons. This becomes obsessive and self-defeating. The answer is really that I have been given the opportunity to see how I can hold myself gently and receive the gifts that struggle has to offer. The real question then is, "Can I become less reactive and more loving?"

When we are in challenging times, we get stressed and caught up in a frenzy of emotions that take us out of our bodies and into our minds and egos. We become reactive and enter survival mode. There is no way to connect with our deeper knowing when we are in this state. When I am consumed with reactivity, I become completely disconnected from my inner guidance, from the intelligence that comes from my heart and my intuition. I make choices that lead me down a road with more challenges. I enter into emotional contracts with people who may hurt me deeply. This is because when I am disconnected from my heart and my body, I can't figure out which door to walk through. I can't find my way.

I use the following three steps to deal with my personal challenges. Finding grace through these times is my life long practice, and I know I will use these steps as long as I am here on this planet because that is precisely how long I will continue to be challenged.

1) Avoid the temptation to bring more drama to the challenge. It is so easy to get frustrated and be pushed to the point of wanting to share your story with everyone, to have outbursts, to throw tantrums or to feel like you are the victim. Instead, practice silence, intentional conversation and contemplation.

2) Being loving does not mean you have to forgive or take abuse from someone or a situation. It means that you do not have to react from a defensive place. If you connect to the love within, you will be able to see that there is struggle in all of us and this can open us up to compassion for others. You can show compassion toward someone else from afar and internally, in your mind and in your body. It does not have to be outwardly expressed to matter.

3) Take a breather. The moment you find yourself being triggered and want to attack, stop yourself. Maybe go for a walk, close your office door (or put in headphones if you don't have a door), breathe, and move away from computers or phones where the temptation to respond can be more acute. Wait an hour. A day. A week. Wait until the charge is gone and you find space within that feels at peace. Every challenge is an opportunity to find your peace.

I have been personally attacked and accused of being someone that I know is not true. I have been accused of unimaginable things, and I have wanted – **needed** – desperately to prove them wrong, to tell them all the ways they are wrong. But here is what I have learned from these experiences: I must respond without defensiveness. I respond from the person that I want to be, the person that I want my actions and my words to show that I am. I respond from my wisdom instead of my ego. I do not try to show how idiotic they may be (to me) because of their inaccuracies or stories. I remember that in some place within them, this hurtful story they are telling is true. It could be from their past, but something has triggered some deep fear within them and it is being poured onto me. But it is not mine. What they say does not have to be my truth. I soften into myself, I cry to release tension, I pray for my heart connection to grown deeper and I gently remove myself from my reactive ego. And I breathe.

## 31

# Are You Wasting Energy Hating Someone?

People Are Hard To Hate Up Close.
Dr. Brené Brown

B rené Brown's research and work is very important in our world, right now and for the future. I want to bring light to some of the things she speaks of and help spread her teachings because I feel privileged to be present on this planet at the same time she is here doing her work.

In her book, *Braving The Wilderness,* Brown talks about how it's hard to hate people up close, and suggests we move in. Get close and see yourself in them. This action results in a profound inner challenge. We make people the enemy from afar. We decide we are somehow different from them. We imagine that we are better, that we would make better decisions if we were in their shoes. Think about how many times you have had thoughts like that. If you are a parent, you know that you thought you would do it differently from others, that somehow you would have more insight. This is only until you become a parent and realize that you are in way over your head and have to figure it all out along the way, just like everyone else. That is, unless you still believe you know the answers and feel called to tell others how to parent (there still are a number of folks out there in that camp). My point is, we don't know what it's like for someone else. We don't know their sufferings or traumas. I like to remind myself that everyone is doing the best they can, even if their best does not match up to mine.

Brown also teaches us that we can be present with people without sacrificing who we are, or at the cost of our freedom, authenticity and power. Wow! Imagine being present without stepping into the Us vs. Them mentality. Imagine knowing that you do not need to make yourself bigger than someone else to be in your power. The power comes from within, and not from dominating someone else. She reminds us that we will "do anything to consume facts that support our point of view". We will find anything to make ourselves right. We will look at facts and change the meaning of them to support how badly we want to be right. We will endorse our beliefs by finding more and more proof that what we are believing is, in fact, truth.

When we are seeing ourselves as separate from others, when we believe that because their opinions are different from ours it makes them wrong. We forget that we all want to be loved, we all want to be seen, we have all endured pain (some more than others) and we are all doing our best. Lean in, have a look deeper into the eyes of those you've made into villains, and see if you can look at them from your heart instead of your mind.

Ask yourself, are you responding from your highest self, and not from the ego that wants to be correct and win? Are you responding from a space within you that can allow for different points of view while still maintaining your own? Can you see that in allowing for other perspectives you can still have your freedom, because your freedom comes from within? Nelson Mandela kept his power during close to three decades in prison because he understood that his happiness and power existed within him, and no one could take that from him. Think about that. He found the capacity to be authentic and remain in his power after almost thirty years in prison. Often we will believe that someone else can take away our power. That in order to remain in control, we have to dominate with our views and opinions. I believe none of us have had to spend three decades in prison by speaking our truths; truths aimed at creating a better world.

Can we stop hating people? Can we look for common ground? Can we empower and teach our children to find the good in others, not teach them to make other people wrong?

This is a hard practice. The ego wants desperately to be in control. Is this a practice you are willing to start looking at?

Because we **all** need compassion.

# 32

## Set Intentions You Can Follow

*If you want to attract something new -- a
relationship, a career -- consider exactly
how you want to feel.*

How can we do this in a way that positions us better for success? How do we follow through instead of letting our will and vision fade out after a couple of weeks?

I believe **how** we set goals is more important than the goals we set. We need to set intentions that are attainable, and this is more easily achieved when we consider how we want to *feel* rather than moving toward goals that leave us feeling empty because they are rooted in the wrong source. Have you ever set an intention like 'lose weight'? And then failed miserably because you hate going to the gym but still assigned yourself five gym workouts a week to meet your goal? If reaching your goals requires you to become a different person (one who suddenly, spontaneously *likes* the gym, for example), chances are you're not going to get far in the process.

Intentions are attainable when they inspire us, like being of service to others or filling our minds with inspired readings by people who keep us on track. Sitting on a stationary bike to burn 500 calories is not inspiring and can be lonely and boring *unless* you can source the energy for your workout from a deeper, more useful place, like knowing your good health will keep you around longer with more energy and allow you to move with ease.

Instead of thinking about what you want, start thinking about how you want to *feel*. The difference is that when you decide how you want to feel, you can move more intuitively toward your goal because you understand the objective on a visceral level. Feeling a new experience in the body is amazing. It feels lighter and enjoyable. It motivates.

If you want to feel healthy and connected to your community, join a group of like-minded individuals and get fit together. You can solicit friends and choose to support each other by setting days and times each week you that will meet up for activities like doing yoga, swimming or going to the gym.

If you want to attract something new, like a relationship or a career, consider exactly how you want to feel. When you are able to get clear about this, you can then spend time imagining what being in a relationship with someone who has those qualities feels like (the opposite would be being fearful of finding someone who will bring in the same issues as you've experienced in past relationships). When you focus on what you don't want, you may end up following that path instead.

To create successful intentions, think about how you want to feel, find ways to get connected with your community and keep company with people who support you.

# 33
## What Gossip Feels Like

People are quick to believe the bad
things they hear about good people.
Unknown

I was a seasoned gossiper. I grew up being shown that in order to engage in the world, I was required to talk about others. Family, friends, political representatives and strangers: I learned to judge them all. To look at everyone else and consider how they may be wrong. Ugg. I was entitled and righteous in my judgments. I felt that to be liked I needed to make myself appear better than others, and I generously offered up examples of all the ways that others were flawed.

I believe gossip became a way of self-defense for me. For years, I watched people (from my family to my immediate and distant social groups) talk about me in ways that were not true. I struggled with their misrepresentation of my true nature. In order to combat the inner battle between my knowledge of myself and the 'Noelle' they talked about but did not know, I joined in. I decided my best defense was to fight by judging and gossiping.

Sometimes the friends that I was sharing my judgments with would buy into my stories, but mostly I felt a blankness from them. They did not have the same emotions attached and couldn't relate; I would try harder to strengthen my case. More often than not, this would send me on a downward spiral of verbal diarrhea that left me and my captured audience feeling depleted.

A few years ago I started a two-fold change:

1) The first step was **gossip detox** – I consciously stopped sharing things that ultimately depleted my self-worth. I began watching myself not say those things I thought I SHOULD share, things that strengthened my lack of self-worth. What I witnessed was a lightening of my experience of myself. I felt less depleted after my conversations and more at peace. I may not have been able to defend myself or my beliefs, but I felt calmer and more grounded. I was curious enough to observe my own reactions to others and myself when I did gossip.

2) I chose a path of moving more cleanly in the world and seeking out people who inspire me to do and be and express my best self (instead of those bring out my bitchy high school self). If I want to create a life of feeling genuinely well inside, I need to allow for higher frequencies of conversation to move through me, meaning I choose to have conversations that feel abundant and exciting as well as stimulate and inspire me. Today I spend most of my life in what inspires me, with people that inspire me (not that I put on a pedestal) and whom I enjoy being around. I cleaned out my company so that I stopped filling those depleted places within me with people who feed on the weaker parts of me.

What I noticed is that there is a difference between speaking up for yourself and gossiping. If I need to work through something – an interaction with someone, or some way that I have felt wronged – I will chat in confidence with one person in order to gain clarity. I ask for guidance, and I try not to diminish the other person involved. In that place, I can make sound, well-guided choices that come from a peaceful place. What I don't do is talk about the same issue with multiple people in order to indulge in the story or make sure it is told in many ways to many people.

I still fall off the gossip wagon and indulge sometimes. But when I do, I know I am doing it. I am selective about those with whom I share. I generally admit what I am doing, and I make sure I don't overindulge. Most of the time, when I jump back onto that well worn pathway of gossip, I feel a sort of hangover. A haze in myself. A lack of inspiration. A darker side of myself which doesn't fill my sense of well-being. Then I have to build my energy back up, the same way you do after drinking too much. I have to carefully select healthy ideas, thoughts and foods to fill my body and mind.

If I want to feel genuinely well inside, I need to allow for higher frequencies of conversation to move through me, meaning I need to have conversations that feel abundant and exciting as well as ones that stimulate and inspire me.

I feel much better because of it.

# 34
# The Power of Our Thoughts

Every thought we think is
creating our future.
Louise Hay

Thoughts are powerful. I believe they create our
reality. I believe thoughts have the capacity to
enlighten us, lift us to higher places and make dreams
come true. They can also tear us to pieces, destroy
dreams and relationships and get the better of us at
the worst possible times.

I used to be prisoner to my thoughts, believing them
to be the absolute truth, believing that my harsh,
internal self-judgment was actually some higher power

keeping me small and in line. My thoughts controlled me. Limited me. They imprisoned me within the boundaries of my body. I couldn't get away from them. They took over like parasites, relentlessly infecting everything in and around me.

My thoughts kept me in bad relationships, kept me from following my heart, kept me from doing what I instinctively knew I should be doing. They kept me from feeling whole and connecting with my inner self. They inspired great sadness and deep loneliness.

One day, I started watching my thoughts, observing that they were very rough and wondering if there might be another way. Could I soften their edges? And how would that change my experience? I imagined my thoughts like a train, brakeless and speeding forward, out of control, headed for only God knows where. I imagined taking my own hand and gently bringing the train to a stop. Then I started the process of backing it up, steering myself with kind, gentle thoughts and watching sweetness guide me back home to the station. Centred, I could remind myself what I actually wanted to be thinking about and how I wanted to feel as a result, and I set off again, intentionally controlling the speed and direction of my travel.

It was a slow process. Eventually I started to watch the train with more diligence. It would go for days or months or years, then I would finally notice that it was out of control and guide it back with as much gentleness as I could muster. With that practice, over time, it became easier and easier to manage my train of thoughts.

I am now the conductor of these thoughts. I watch them as they leave the station, and when I notice thoughts that don't serve me, I pull them back as quickly as I can. Some are harder to catch than others, but overall, this awareness brings wisdom to my experience. Instead of feeling reckless and wild, my thoughts are laced with positivity, possibility, inspiration, love and a knowing that I am meant for peace.

When I find my thoughts are guided by someone else's opinions, by some sense of worthlessness I've picked up from looking at Facebook or inexplicably sourced in my own self doubt, I know I am capable of reminding myself that no one but me is responsible for how I think. I fully understand the relationship between my thoughts and my emotions: if I am mindful of the thoughts I am consuming, I can position myself to enjoy the good and great feelings they produce without leaving room to indulge in the ones that bring me into a deep pool of misery.

It's been an amazing transformation in my life.

What thoughts will guide you today?

# 35

# Living a Life of Never Enough

I'm still learning to love the parts
of myself that no one claps for.
Ruby Francisco

Do you feel the pull of 'never enough'? Never enough time, sleep, money, sex, work, beauty, patience, success, exercise, healthy choices and so on. Do you feel like no matter what you do, it's never good enough? Do you feel that you are juggling so many roles – parent, student, wife, partner, caregiver, housekeeper, teacher, mentor, breadwinner, musician, professional – that every role you have you're unable to give 100%? Are you living a constant iteration of running on the treadmill of 'never enough'?

Our world has changed so much. Never in our history have we had so much connection with our immediate and not so immediate communities. Never before have we been able to share our lives with the world at the click of a finger. We have moved into a new way of interacting with our global community and we are in the infancy of this era. We are the guinea pigs. We cannot learn how to navigate these unfamiliar waters from any example in history. It is hard to fully understand how this will define our culture and our future as humans.

We have become attached to small computers that update us day and night on what is happening in everyone else's lives. We are inundated with images of the best moments of others' lives as they endlessly display their successes. Overindulging in selfies and narcissistic behavior only encourages more self-indulgent behavior. My intention is not to attack; I am simply observing the changes I've seen in our world.

With these constant social affronts, we tend to be more and more judgmental. We judge others and their choices. We decide, by what they show us, that they are better than us and their lives matter more because they have more money, more freedom to play, more ability to travel and, ultimately, more reasons to be loved. It feels like whatever we are doing is not enough to keep up with everyone else's excellent lives.

What if you chose to hold back from showing your life to the world? Do you feel like you would disappear into the great unknown, that somehow you'd be forgotten? That you'd be 'unliked'? That your life wouldn't matter?

What would happen if you were able to pull back the self-judgement? Would it mean you would judge others less? Feel more balanced in your own life? In my experience, the answer is 'yes'.

Problems arise when we live without examining our behaviors or our reactions to what we are seeing. An unexamined life leads to behaviors that lack social and moral consciousness. We jump almost blindly onto social media as a form of self-punishment. You know you'll turn it off feeling a little less whole than when you opened it, but you indulge nonetheless. It's destructive. And exhausting. So why do we do it?

When someone posts something that's cringe-worthy, it's like a car accident: we can't help but gawk. You want to look away, but you can't.

It's easy to jump into the idea that in order to be liked, we need to post more, show more. Yet this leaves us feeling less and less connected to what truly matters to us. How do we navigate the waters of not pretty enough, not loved enough, not affluent enough, not patient enough? Moving from this place, we cannot help but lack appreciation and gratitude for all the gifts we already have.

Yet we have opportunity in the unknown. We can direct our outcomes. There is hope. We can dream up where we want to go, how we want to relate to and in this world and how we want to teach our children to interact and respond to the endless stimulation.

I believe the answers lie in the questions we ask. What do you want for your future? What relationships do you want to nourish? How do you want to connect to your community? How do you want to feel? What skills do you want your children to have (not technical skills, but emotional skills). How do you want to influence the future with your actions, not for fame but for emotional well-being?

These questions help guide us away from the feeling of not being enough. When we stop looking outward to see what everyone else is doing we feel more grounded, less controlled by the devil of comparison and more connected to a life that is authentic to us.

# 36
# What Does it Mean to Be Spiritual?

Stay in the spiritual fire. Let it cook you.
Rumi

It's a question that is often asked to the thought leaders of our time: "What does spirituality mean to you?" To me, spirituality is tuning into a higher awareness within. It doesn't have to be some esoteric connection to the great unknown (mind you, I love connecting with the great unknown), but rather an understanding that it is worth asking, "What else is there"? Here are my eight practices of what being spiritual means:

1) **Spirituality is about asking questions**. Spirituality is about being conscious. It is about asking questions instead of just accepting what others tell you. If you're reading this, you've had a moment in your life when you wanted to know more, when you stopped acting without thought and started getting interested in your unanswered questions. Spirituality is about getting curious and knowing that there are questions within you that are worth asking and seeking. It is about becoming an inner seeker.

2) **Spirituality means thinking about how you respond to the world**, and paying attention to the ways in which you respond. It is about being curious enough to ask if the ways you respond are serving you. It means finding the teacher within, and using your experiences to educate and inform you. It means using your life as the great Guru - your life is your teacher. I like to say that I am doing my PhD in myself. I am uncovering my worn-out beliefs and choosing to look at what feels like an authentic expression of myself, rather than doing what I think others want me to do. It is about getting real with myself, and owning my mistakes. Spirituality is choosing to no longer hide from myself.

3) **Spirituality means taking ownership of yourself and no longer blaming others.** I loved to blame others! It was the ultimate guilty pleasure: it meant I didn't have to own any of my own experiences. But guess what? If you are choosing to be a proactive agent in your life, you soon become aware that responding with indignant blame gets you nowhere. Blame only creates shame, a deep shame of swirling

unhappiness. So I stopped. My experiences are my own, and I practice not taking on the truths of others. When others attempt to place blame on me, I am tempted to sink into shame again. But than I remind myself, "Hey! You don't blame others for your own experience, so you don't need to take that from someone else." So, as a practice, I choose to let it go.

4) **Spirituality is choosing to stop indulging in drama.** Another way I that **loved** to respond to the world was with drama. I loved it, and if I could hang out in it, I never had to think about what was really happening in my world. I could just keep creating or interacting with dramas as a measure of self-importance. You know, the kind of importance that gave me permission to not connect with myself. I was shamefully good at it. I had to let go to realize a love for myself, and to move toward a feeling of inner peace.

5) **Spirituality is letting go of the need to control.** I had to let go of the need to control and trust that I could accept whatever came my way. A need to control consumed me, and I would react when **anything** got in the way of my plans. I would feel pinched by anxiety wanting to control everything around me. Like all the other practices, I had to stop trying to control. Even when others were trying to control me, I had to let go of the need to respond with the same fear. Control often means that things need to go your way for you to feel safe in the world whether it is in your life or whether that includes the lives of those around you. So look at the ways in which you need control.

6) **Spirituality is trusting in things you can't explain.** I trust. Now more than ever, I trust in the magic that happens around me. I trust in the power of waiting for the answers or responding from my gut. I trust in the power of prayers. I trust in the power of intention. I trust in a love greater than I currently know. I trust in allowing for things to come, instead of trying to control outcomes. I trust in what I am being taught. I trust in my instincts. I trust in the things I can't prove but know to be true. I trust beyond any comprehension. I trust beyond a need to control. I trust I have what it takes to guide me through any challenge that life presents. I just trust.

7) **Spirituality is avoiding the temptation to judge.** We judge it all day long; we judge our environment and those around us. A judgement detox can help clear the ways we all judge. When we judge someone else for doing the best they can with their current set of skills, we close ourselves off, and we are unable to see their light or the gifts they can offer. If we soften the outer judge, we can also soften the inner critic, who is likely the most brutal critic.

8) **Spirituality means building an inner resilience**, a resilience that can help you during your storms and serve you in a deeply sacred way. It gives you the power to be the commander of your own ship, and reminds you that you get to choose from a deep wisdom within as opposed to having unconscious outbursts. And if you do have those outbursts, you can find the strength within to right your ship. Resilience allows for the capacity to navigate anything that comes your way, and is often built by those who choose to learn from their experience.

I am not the same person I was 10 years ago, and I imagine I will say that in another 10 years. I've learned not to act blindly in the world. I don't want to be the same person I am today in a decade. I choose to be mindful of myself. I realize that I can choose to pay attention to my own thoughts and that they don't own me. My thoughts help show me what I believe of myself; my thoughts can be brutal at times. Being spiritual means trusting in the power of loving myself in order to be of greater service to my friends and loved ones. My spiritual practice has taught me that responding from love wins over responding from anger, fear and the need to be right.

# 37

## Do You Want to Be Happier?

Keep choosing happiness daily, and
happiness will keep choosing you back.
Fawn Weaver

Where do you believe your happiness level is at? Are you a super happy person most of the time, or do you feel like you need to work on happiness? Do you know that the level of happiness you may feel at any given time is a genetic gift, meaning that it is something you are born with? There has been a number of scientific studies done to help us understand happiness. One study, published in the *Journal of Personality* and done by the University of Edinburgh in Scotland, suggests that up to half the happiness we feel can be attributed to genetic makeup. The research participants had a number of personality traits that made them drawn to feeling happier, including the ability to accept themselves.

Culturally there seems to be a trend to desire or quest for happiness. Happiness appears to be a birthright, something we feel entitled to. But are we? Are we supposed to be granted a level of happiness that disconnects us from our heartaches and challenges? I don't think so. I believe that there is an overarching goal of happiness that seems to be taking over our social networks. Just open Facebook, Instagram or any other social media platform and you will see endless displays of apparent happiness. But are the actors really as happy as they appear? Are you really as happy as you show the world...or even your friends and family?

In order to search for happiness, we must allow ourselves to feel that it is OK to not be happy every single day. That feeling crappy is also OK. Have you ever tried to hide a deep sadness from a dear friend for fear of being judged that you may be less desirable if you are not exuding a certain level of positivity? That you should look for the good in everything that comes your way? Have you ever found yourself saying, "well the good in this is...". or "at least I learned..."? How about, "look at the bright side..."? Look at the language we use just so we don't have to admit our true feelings.

In order to have a real conversation with yourself about happiness, you need to first establish what brings you joy. What do you enjoy doing? Do you enjoy being of service to others? Going for a run? Reading a good book? Eating lovingly prepared food? Hanging out with your lover or snuggling with your kids? Cleaning your house? Going to a party? Making space for people that you enjoy being around? Sleeping in? Cleaning out your fridge once a week? Finally tackling your 'to do' list? If we spend our time avoiding the things that make us happy, because we feel that there are more important things we need to be attending to, our happiness lags. Eventually you may look at your life and wonder how you've wandered so far away from feeling good.

I used to believe that I didn't have space for pleasure, and that it was an indulgent behavior. I realized that thinking was a little backwards, and that if I didn't allow for enjoyment, how could I possibly show up in a joyful way for others?

Look around at those who seem happy and ask them how they fill their days. You will likely discover that they fill themselves up with what **they** enjoy, and not with what others think they should be doing. It's going to be a challenge to actualize a feeling of happiness within if you are not sure what makes you happy, or if you're living for others' desires.

There is a baseline of happiness we need to create in order to reach that feeling in our day to day life. For myself, having an organized home and office gives me great satisfaction. For most of us, what happens on the outside is happening on the inside, so a calm outer world brings great inner peace. I make sure I prioritize things that bring me pleasure in my life.

I feel great joy when I make my bed before I leave the house in the morning. Having healthy nutritious food in my fridge makes me feel abundant. Making time to get exercise makes me happy and promotes creativity. Spending quality time with my daughter is one of the best parts of my day. Being present with my lover. I have a gratitude practice that has become habitual. I take breathes in many moments of my day when I am grateful for the little things in my life, the people, conversations, smiles, sunshine, snow, rain and scents. A healthy dose of gratitude is the cherry on the top of your happiness scale.

When I stack all those things together, my baseline is filled up. That way when something happens in my life that is disappointing, I am already feeling full and it cannot pull me into despair. You see, if your baseline is running on empty, any event in your life can leave you feeling disappointed and depleted.

So, what would it take to make yourself happier today? What parts of yourself are screaming for a little attention? What are the small things that make you feel great? Take stock of those things and make them the ingredients that create your happy life. Allow for your baseline to move above the line of feeling depleted. From there, you can add extras like vacations, dream expeditions, social dates and party invitations. The extras feel more deluxe when your baseline is already filled and you'll be able to enjoy those moments with even more gratitude.

# 38

# Courage Is the Most Important Virtue

Courage doesn't mean you don't get afraid.
Courage means you don't let fear stop you.
Unknown

Our virtues define who we are and how we are remembered. They also guide our present and future experiences. The list of virtues is extensive and includes authenticity, compassion, confidence, encouragement, forgiveness, gratitude, joy, love, optimism, truth and so many more. However, none of these virtues are possible without courage. Courage allows us to harness the powers of all the other virtues.

Courage allows us to move through pain. It allows us to decide that there is a space on the other side of whatever we've been through that can be more gentle and spacious than where we began. Courage moves us toward the magic. Many of us will do anything to remain within our comfort zones, even if that place is built from pain. Familiarity trumps actual comfort. Any movement out of what we know can feel scary. Courage is what allows us to take action, and what pushes us through the dark times with an inner knowing, even if – or maybe **especially if** – the hardest times are our best teachers. If you can endure pain long enough to see the light beyond it, and if you can move forward in spite of the hurt and resistance, you will, with certainty, emerge into a better world.

Are you conducting yourself with courage?

Courage is what allows love to prosper in our lives. We have all been hurt, by a lover, family or friend. It takes courage to let go of pain and move toward love, a love that isn't limited by the fear of being hurt again. A love that speaks to our deepest fears and reminds us that even if we are hurt again, we will be OK. A love that reminds us that it can feel so good it is worth taking the risk of choosing love over obsessing about what could go wrong. A love that holds your heart so deeply, you know you have the capacity to heal yourself, no matter what. Hurt may be inevitable, but your recovery is just as sure a thing if you can remain courageous in the face of what you fear.

Courage is the power that allows us to move any mountains in our way. It allows us to apply for jobs, to submit books to 200 different publishes, to go on the trip of a lifetime, to start a business, to try a new sport, to eat something new, to have a new perspective, to change a limiting pattern, to leave a marriage, to have children, to not have children, to pick up and start all over again even when you've lost everything.

If you move into courage, you push beyond your own limitations; with a steady practice, you will begin to increase the range of comfortable activity. Over time, you'll find that the old, scary place of the unknown has become a beautiful and easy place for you to explore and work. You learn, you grow and you age, and with that there is grace and expansion.

It takes courage to say YES or to say NO. It takes courage to be kind when someone is unkind to you. It takes courage to be generous with your time when you would rather hide. It takes courage to speak your truth without an undertone of forcefulness. It takes courage to stop indulging in relationships that are clearly harmful for you. It takes courage to get quiet and stop moving so fast. It take courage to understand someone else's perspective, even when it is opposite to your own. It takes courage not to judge.

Are you ready to create the life you want to be living? Ready to move into a new emotional state? To take a step toward what you have been dreaming about for so long? Even if you don't feel you embody the virtue of courage, if you do something that requires you to be courageous, you will begin the process of building virtue.

How are you going to be courageous today?

# 39

# Why Is it So Hard to Forgive?

The weak can never forgive. Forgiveness
is the attribute of the strong.
Mahatma Gandhi

To forgive is one of the most challenging things we
can do. Holding onto resentment often feels 'right',
as though holding onto it gives us permission to be
hurt. We can convince ourselves that the person who
hurt us must not be forgiven because if we forgive, we
would be saying, "It's OK that you hurt me." The thing
is, the only person that is hurt when we don't forgive
is ourselves. Truly. No one else suffers more deeply
than us.

Sometimes our friends and family suffer because we carry our hurt like a badge honoring our pain. We may have the illusion that convincing our closest allies of our pain will help protect us and make the offender suffer. But that is not true. I have learned that my allies tend to turn on me when I spend too much time reasoning why my (perceived) enemy should become theirs, too. Even if you don't feel this resistance from your friends, trying to convince others that someone should be shamed will bring you more pain and more loneliness; you're moving from your smallest self when you're leading a charge like that.

Not forgiving is wanting for a different past. However, it is 100% impossible to go back in time, What is possible is to create the future that you want. If you want to have wholehearted connections and to not feel bound and contracted by your pain, forgiveness is the only way. Forgiveness truly sets us free. It delivers us from our own evils, and from the stories that bind us and keep us small.

Forgiveness is a deeply generous offering to our own journey. Forgiveness says, "I know I was hurt, but it is time to let it go. Not because I am forgiving the behavior or event, but because I am choosing to forgive a being for my own salvation." The less hurt we hold in our own hearts, the more we will be able to offer ourselves, wholeheartedly, to the people and things in our lives that truly matter.

Less pain = softer heart
Softer heart = room to grow into the bright lights we are meant to be

Bright light = peace, both for ourselves and for those around us

It's all a matter of choice. I have held onto pain so tightly, I couldn't breathe. It dictated all of my relationships and experiences. It confined me and kept me small. Once I started to forgive, I had the tremendous experience of living lighter, of literally glowing from the inside out. Of being more at peace, and less at war.

There is so much war on this planet. If we want that to change, we literally have to change the inner wars raging in our hearts. We need to soften to ourselves, to choose a different experience. Forgiveness is not easy, yet once we choose to forgive, it is amazing how everything gets easier.

Forgiveness releases tension, softens stress and has tremendous healing powers.

Trust me, whatever you're holding onto is worth letting go. The freedom is all yours to experience.

Forgiveness is freedom.

# 40

## When Love Doesn't Feel Good

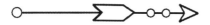

You have to keep breaking
your heart until it opens.
Rumi

Loving is traditionally thought of as an outward expression of feelings. It is rarely (from my perspective) thought of an inward action. The amount we can love someone else is truly dependant on the amount we are able to love ourselves. Sometimes our love for another can feel so intense, it is as though we might implode from the feelings it induces. It can feel like we are losing control because we feel so much towards someone else.

I think love can feel overwhelming when we feel more love flowing out than we hold for ourselves. I can now see that at some points in my life my love was a projection of what I wanted instead of what I had cultivated within. Loving someone else was a method of consumption. Consuming that intense rush of 'love' and experiencing the pheromones that pushed me outside of myself and wrapped me tediously around another provided me with the illusion that I was special. In fact, it just made me feel terrified that those feelings would not be reciprocated.

When we are unable to love ourselves with as much ferocity as we love another, it can feel destabilizing. This is because we aren't actually able to love ourselves with this same intensity, and when we devote all our love to someone else we begin to lose our connections to ourselves. At least I know this to be true for myself.

When I have fallen into that deep 'head over heals' kind of love with someone, it comes with a powerful sense of not being worthy of receiving that same kind of love. I feel it is because I haven't been able to love myself and I am afraid of losing myself when I lose that love. It is a truly ungrounded feeling and keeps me destabilized in myself.

Finding my own love has been a great adventure, one that is far from over. I have learned that I will be OK when things fall apart in my heart. I also have learned that the amount I am willing to love myself directly affects my sense of worthiness.

How much are you able to love yourself? How do we measure the amount of love we give to ourselves? Is that even possible?

True love is kind, generous, patient and vulnerable. It has clear boundaries. True love allows us to be us, have our own lives and learn to cocreate with someone else. It isn't something that eats up our whole being and makes two into one. It unites our differences and teaches us to explore our boundaries and our ego's desire to control.

When we are scared to be open to our own truths and fears about love, we are unable to be honest with someone else. We will always seek control, because we are controlling ourselves. I did this for years; I was controlling so I would feel like I was in the driver's seat and could manage 'them' and in turn feel like I could manage myself.

Not being able to give yourself fully to someone is simply liking them from a distance. Wanting to be with someone but holding back is self-protective; we are not sharing ourselves. It keeps people at arms length so we don't have to open the Pandora's Box of our hearts. The fear of emotion can be so overwhelming I think most of us spend our whole lives avoiding that kind of depth with another person in order to control our sensory world.

Are you able to listen to someone wrestle with their own pain, or do you need to interject with your own insights? Do you find yourself changing the subject because it makes you uncomfortable to listen? These are strong indicators that you are not able to love yourself.

Are you a runner? Someone who avoids intimacy or opening your heart to someone? Do you feel you need to remain closed so that you don't ever have to succumb to being hurt? Does your pain from the past keep you from opening your heart at all? This can play out in a long term relationships when you choose not to share your emotions because you are worried about how your partner will respond or when you convince yourself you 'know' how they will respond so you begin to self edit in order to remain in control of outcome.

Perhaps you are more intellectual about your love: Do you rationalize and strategize your approach about how you will manage yourself when you are hurt? Do you talk about it with your friends, even explain in detail why something didn't work out, but feel almost numb to the feelings?

If we feel like victims we tend to run; when we feel like we are smart enough to use our intellect to manage our hearts we disconnect from love.

Watch the ways in which you respond outwardly to love as these will be indicative of how much you are allowing yourself to love yourself.

My humble offering, if you are struggling with loving yourself, is to suggest you focus on building that relationship before delving too deeply into committing to something you are unable to show up for 100%.

# 41

# Positivity Holds A Higher Vibration

If you realized how powerful your
thoughts were you'd never think
another negative thought again.
Unknown

D o you ever feel that being positive is a passive
behavior? Do you feel that being positive can
make you clueless to the obvious? Maybe positive
people piss you off. Or perhaps being positive feels
natural and immediate to you.

I love being optimistic. It is, however, a practice. I work
diligently to see the bright side. I believe this is part of

creating inner peace, and it helps me lean toward the positive side of things.

There are times I fall off the positive mindset wagon and sink into despair. In these moments, I have to remind myself to not get self-critical about feeling negative: sometimes we just need to sit in the dark. It offers us an important perspective and allows us to see and **feel** the difference between positive and negative thoughts.

A good observational practice is to ask yourself which you indulge in more, optimism or pessimism? If you can remember that where your attention goes, energy flows, then you can understand the importance of being discerning about where you rest your focus.

I believe all of us (or almost all of us) can feel the vibration someone else is holding. It can feel positive or negative, it can feel high or low. Essentially, your gut is your information centre, and it informs you. When you run into someone at the grocery store, and have a little chat, you may pick up on a dark cloud feeling from them. Or a bright, light one.

Here is what I know for sure: positivity holds a higher vibration than negativity. As cited by Earth Unchained (an online resource), "When 2 frequencies come together, the lower one rises to meet the higher". This means we should always aim to seek higher vibrational thoughts and actions.

What kind of vibration are you offering to the world? Is your cup half empty, or half full?

Regardless of where you are on the spectrum of positivity, how do you raise your vibration when you are struck by a negative cord? Those times that feel challenging and really push you are the ones that challenge you on the deepest level. Those times offer us the greatest opportunities to do our work. So how do you shift toward the positive?

I am not saying that we ignore the negative or attempt to avoid it. If you do that, you will be disconnected from the situation. When we **force** ourselves into being positive we gloss over our true feelings. We disconnect from ourselves.

It's possible to allow **both to be present**. You have the option to choose which path you want to follow.

You can **choose** to spend more time looking for positive solutions rather than remain fixed on negative outcomes. You have the choice to be positive even when the situation isn't. It doesn't mean you wear blinders or spew positivity; it means that you don't get caught in the tempting drama of what being negative brings.

It's when we downplay a situation (or gloss it over) that if things don't work out the way we had hoped, we get taken out at the ankles (emotionally speaking).

Through experience, you can step away from indulging in the negative and become more observant of how feeling positive can lift you up. It can help you be kinder and more generous, not only to yourself but to all those involved.

# 42

# Is It Possible Everything Is Happening for You?

Most people do not realize that the
challenges they experience in their
life, are there for a spiritual reason.
Deepak Chopra

How much time have you wasted blaming life events and situations on other people?

It took me a long time to recognize the benefits of the 'painful events' in my life. These events were happening for me, not to me. These experiences have helped shape me into the person I am today. I have become more trusting, patient and generous, as well as a stronger and kinder person. I used to blame others for my experiences. I gave away my power, because I felt like I had to have control when I believed a story to be an affront to the sovereignty of my inner peace. It took time for me to digest the idea that everything was happening 'for' me, instead of 'to' me.

What if your broken heart was teaching you that you are capable of loving again, even after being hurt? If someone has broken a bond of trust, this is not teaching you not to trust again, but perhaps to be more discerning in whom you trust. The lesson could be the recognition that your self-worth isn't dictated by the person who hurt you. You can trust yourself to make different choices as you move forward. If you lose someone close, the lesson is not to be guarded and stop living, but rather to recognize the infinite connection we have with loved ones, even when they are not here on Earth. This lesson might guide you to become more joyful and take more risks; it is understanding that this life is precious.

There is a lot of talk about the law of attraction these days, but I believe the interpretation of it can be misguided. If something doesn't come easily to you, or if you don't get that job, or that date, it is not the universe trying to tell you that it is not right for you. But it may be an opportunity for you to decide how much you want it, and whether you are willing to work hard and put in time to work toward your goal.

There are times when it doesn't work out for the better, but there are also times when we are called to stand taller and believe in ourselves with more fierceness if we are to achieve what we want in life.

Either way, it's not about believing the choice is out of your hands; it is choosing to see that you have a choice. Whether it is the direction you want to go, or how much you are going to give of yourself or that you can choose to let it go, the power is all within you.

The stories that make up your life are here to teach you. The dramas, heartaches, loves, challenges, joys, as well as the courage, vulnerability and expectations are all offerings. They are on offer so you can trust yourself, rather than assume you have no control. Recognize that you are not here to hold onto the reins of life and get tossed around, but to find your way gracefully on the seat of your journey, and to choose to harness your power instead of giving it away.

I see it often: good people dealing with hard experiences in life, and blaming others for their experiences, even years later. They give over their sense of worthiness, and choose to feel dark inside because they have decided that blaming someone else is more important than looking at what was gifted to them. We struggle to see that life is happening for us when we live in a defensive place and believe things are happening to us.

Someone else's judgement of you is an opportunity to become more of who you are, and to trust in yourself more than in the opinions and judgments of others. Their judgement is not your truth, unless you make it so.

It is time to choose wisely, to begin to shift perspective. To see how to stop giving away control, and become softer and more awake in your own experiences. To regain your inner balance by giving up the sense of control you get from blaming others and own your own experiences.

There is no time like the present.

## 43

# What It Means to Be a Genuine Friend

Friends are medicine for a wounded
heart, and vitamins for a hopeful heart.
Steve Marobili

What does friendship mean to you? What qualities come to mind when you think of a dear friend? How do your friends show up for you? How do you show up for your friends? Do your friendships feel supportive and expansive? Do they allow you to make mistakes, or do they shun you when you've failed? Can you trust them with your soft, raw places? Can they show up for you when you're ready to celebrate an accomplishment that is a long time in the making?

Listen: we can only have a small handful of really close, dear friends. It's very rare to be able to hold space (and time) for more. What I have learned is that we may only have one to four close friendships at once. It takes time, attention and *intention* to build the trust and strong bonds that deep friendships are made of, and they take real tending and patience to stay healthy. For most of us, while the results are well worth the output, we can't invest this fully in everyone we know (and like!). It simply wouldn't be sustainable.

A friend is someone whom you can call when things are falling apart, when you need someone to listen to you. Someone that helps remind you that you are not alone in the world. Henri Nouwen says that a friend who cares deeply, rather than giving advice, solutions or cures, will instead choose "to share our pain and touch our wounds with a warm and tender hand. The friend who can be silent with us in a moment of despair or confusion, who can stay with us in an hour of grief and bereavement, who can tolerate not knowing, not curing, not healing, and face with us the reality of our powerlessness, that is a friend who cares."

Showing up for a friend doesn't mean you smile, nod and say, "That sucks!" and then move on. Or avoid them when things aren't so pretty. Showing up for a friend means being present in the discomfort. It's easy to show up for someone when they are joyful and abundant with fun stories and lovely tales of travel. Only someone with a solid inner character can show up when life is not pretty. Showing up when there is ugliness is real, even if it's difficult. You still find the strength within to show up for someone else that needs it. Even if that means sitting together, with tissues, a bottle of wine and a movie, just sitting. Or maybe you choose to sleep over and show your solidarity by just being there. Words aren't always required. Sometimes things are so desperately raw that all you can do is hold your friend, or be held by them.

Showing up also means that when you are not personally full of joy, you still show up to celebrate a milestone or a major life transition. Sometimes you need to remember that it's worth taking yourself out of your own experience to be there for someone else.

How do you want to be nurtured in your darkest times? Think of that when someone else is struggling. Meet your dearests where you may one day want to be met. Or at the very least, try not to cower. Show up, even if it means being silent. Show up even if it means putting aside your own struggles to celebrate someone else's successes. Showing up is what binds friends together. It is how we are able to determine if a friend is worth putting the energy into.

How are you showing up for your friends?

# 44

# Learn to Heal by Loving Yourself

Loving ourselves works miracles in our lives.
Louise Hay

I believe that the deepest love we are meant to feel is for ourselves. I believe that if we can cultivate a real, deep love for ourselves, we can develop the strength for change. We can develop the capacity to forgive the unforgivable. We can change minds with love; we can create peace with love. We can find an empathy that shatters judgement. We can unite with those we've felt distance. Love can hold us with such courage that we find ourselves braving things we've never imagined. *We can heal ourselves with love.*

A love that comes from within has gentleness. A love from within forgives on the deepest level, right down to the soul. It is also the most concentrated and profound practice because it requires a commitment to flow with both our deep sorrows and wild happiness.

When we lack self-love, we live in fear, judgement, anger and pain. We lack empathy, we need to be right or in control and we live with these qualities and tend to embrace them as virtues. We live in a world where we feel we need to be better than others, and we become more cynical and less compassionate as a result. That is what we show the world. However, these are not virtues; they disempower and disconnect us from those we hold most dear. Living without inner love isolates us from connecting with others in a meaningful way. We keep relationships on a superficial level because we are unable to connect with ourselves in the deepest ways.

A deep inner love creates inner and outer peace, genuine patience for someone else's struggles and the capacity to be filled with compassion. We are able to be kind and loving to others. We then take that into the world. Fueled by love, we become advocates for great change. We become soldiers of peace by being peaceful. We become an army of kindness by exuding kindness. We become what we practice.

If you are struggling with what is happening in the world, if you want to see more peace in the world, if you want to find a way to make changes (big or small), if you are tired of the hate and divisiveness that is taking over social commentary, then it's time to build love. If you live with an inner environment of distress, discontent, distraction and disconnection from others, then it's time to build the love within.

We heal with love. We heal when we are able to forgive, and forgiveness comes from the gentleness that love brings.

I have discovered the power of self-love. I am a humble student of self-love, in the infantile stage. Self-love involves many parts. It is not as simple as saying, "I love myself" and moving on, especially if you don't **feel** it.

Building love is multifaceted. But it is possible. There are daily practices that can help build the greatest love you will ever know. Here are a few that have helped – and continue to help – me (I recommend trying one to three at a time, so as not to be overwhelmed):

**Meditation**: find time to be quiet and sit still. Your mind may not be quiet, but the space around you is quiet. You will learn that the chatter of your mind is part of navigating the practice of meditation. You will learn to be quiet in the moments between your thoughts. Use guided meditations based on building love.

**Self-care:** put effort into how you show up each day, even in the privacy of your own home

**Fresh air:** even if you only have five minutes, get outside and smell the air. Take five to ten deep breaths. Every day.

**Look:** at yourself in the mirror. Say, "I love you." When you get caught up in self-defeating ideas of the way you think you should look, repeat, "I love you."

**Surround** yourself with people whom you enjoy being around.

**Exercise**: Where I live, most people are pretty darn active, getting out and playing hard. If that is you, make time for mindful physical practices that are gentler and less aggressive, like yoga. Try a Yin-style practice that is slower and complements your lifestyle. If you don't have a lot of time to be active, set yourself up in group classes, whether it's a spin class or yoga, and allow for a mix of yin and yang practices.

**Gratitude**: every day, look at the things you are most grateful for.

**Laugh**: out loud, every day, or as often as you can.

**Develop:** a healthier relationship with technology and social media. Stop watching it all the time.

**Prayer**: pray for guidance in any way that you are seeking it.

My newest practice, and one that has reinvigorated my practice of self-love, is determining what I want to feel on any given day. To do so, decide on the feelings you want to experience for the day/week/month. Write them down and put them on your mirror. Look at them every day. Imagine them when you are met with challenges throughout your day.

Most importantly, do more of what you want to do and less of what you don't want to do.

Bring all your attention to loving yourself. To accomplish the change we want in our lives and in the world, we **all** need to start with the practice of self-love. It will heal deep wounds, and in that healing, old pain will unravel and we will move into new light. This will change our worlds, and bleed out to the bigger world.

# 45

## Is Your Life Beautifully Full
## or Desperately Busy?

In order to live a beautiful life, you must see
how beautiful your life is.

I need to be honest: for a long time my life was
desperately busy. The desperation set in after
I started my business and had my daughter. I was
desperate for so many things: sleep, support, more
time, affection and understanding (at home and work)
I was so consistently overwhelmed that I couldn't keep
up with the demands of my life; it made me dishevelled
and possibly even incompressible at times.

It came on for me suddenly because having a child makes for dramatic changes in a person's life. However, there are times in any of our lives that we get pushed to the busy zone, pedal to the metal, and have to scramble to keep up. Before we are even aware of what is happening we can find ourselves in a frenetic state of constantly chasing. It becomes a habit.

Maybe we are chasing social gatherings, work, family, recreation time, spiritual practices, or social media. We may find ourselves chasing the time it takes to eat well or the time we need connect in deeper ways with our loved ones. We could be chasing date nights or the opportunity to make more money.

My question for you is, do you feel like you have a beautifully full life or a desperately busy one? I spent years in the latter, and as a kid I recall my mother being there constantly. I began to resent myself and the constant feeling I had of not being enough. I was convinced that if I could just keep running myself ragged I would get closer to finding more ease in my life. In fact, the opposite was happening: I was getting spun out, less connected and more anxious.

I decided to make a dramatic change. I decided to change the way I viewed my days and my 'to do' lists. I had to find a way to slow down and lose my addiction to being anxious. This has been a process, and I want to be clear about that because any behaviour that gives us an emotional reward that drives our lives can become an addiction. We can easily become consumed with wanting to attach ourselves to things that keep us in an addictive visceral response.

My first shift was to identify my behaviour and decide that I wanted a new reality. My second shift was to immediately change my response to my days. What I mean is that I had to stop leaving my house in the morning feeling like I was already behind. I began to repeat to myself that, "I have enough time" and remind myself not to believe the inner voice that wanted me to feel stressed. I had to let that go. Every time I started to get caught up in my stress/anxious response I would catch myself, stop and breathe. I would repeat the phrase, "I have enough time" and stay in the moment until the anxiety passed.

Over the last few years of developing this practice, my life is no longer the same mess it was. I have a full life, but my life doesn't run me. My 'to do' lists sometimes feel BIG but I remind myself that I have chosen them, and I question my choices. Do they fill me up? If any of them don't, I remove them from my list. Although there are things that need to be accomplished in life, we can choose to eliminate those that do not have value or do not serve our lives in any way.

Making this choice has actually meant that I am able to see more friends and attend more social events. It means I can connect more intimately with people around me because I have more mental bandwidth to take in more relevant data, rather than filling my life with stuff that clutters my mind and my capacity to engage with the world.

Sure, at times I am still too busy to connect with friends and sometimes I get overwhelmed at work, but I don't let those moments take over my life. I hunker down and take care of the things that need tending to and eventually I come out of it. I watch my addictive tendency to create stress. I stay mindful about how many commitments I make in my life.

I am more fully present in my life than I have ever been.

What about you? Do you feel overrun by your life? Do you feel like you have no control over it? Does your life control you? Do you look at other people and resent the way they get to live their lives?

Or do you feel content? Do you feel happiness during your days? Are you the one who leads your life and gets to make the choices?

Whether you believe it or not, you have the privilege of creating your life. So how are you going to use that privilege to serve yourself and possibly others?

# 46

## How to Tap into Your Intuition

Learn to let your intuition – gut – instinct –
tell you when the food, relationship, the
job isn't good for you (and conversely
when what you're doing is just right).
Oprah Winfrey

Intuition is an elusive concept to a lot of people.
It isn't tangible, it isn't concrete and there is no
science that can help us understand it completely. Yet
you are still likely to be curious about it: "How do I
tap into my intuition? How do I trust it? What does it
feel like? Is it real?"

Intuition can be defined as a gut instinct, an inner knowing or something you feel or hear within yourself. It is defined in the dictionary as "the ability to understand something immediately, without the need for conscious reasoning." (*OED n.1*)

The concept of intuition feels elusive because our minds want to take control and let reason govern our choices and responses. Our minds are built to process rational beliefs; they are designed to undermine what we know to be true, especially if it is unquantifiable by the paradigms through which we are taught and conditioned to 'understand' our world.

Intuition is something that takes time to build. It is developed through a greater understanding and trust of the self. It grows when you learn from your own choices and decisions. You begin to recognize when you haven't listened to your instincts, when there was a knowing, a clue or a tip that you ignored. It is a wisdom that gets developed through age and experience. It is an intelligence that matures through life, and with experience comes clarity. We have to get to know and trust ourselves in the same way we do with those around us. Our ideas of who we are and what we want shift and evolve over time. Intuition is the opposite of holding on to who you think you are, who you think you should be or what you think need. Intuition asks us to let go of the way we **think** things should be and to trust that there is something greater at play that we may not understand or want to hear. Wisdom doesn't have to make sense: it asks us to trust in the journey instead of holding onto old ideas.

I know that if I am heavily emotionally connected to something, or dealing with strong emotions in any form, I am unable to hear my intuition clearly. My thoughts will sabotage my inner wisdom. I recognize that sometimes I don't have the answers because there are other parts of me that I can't fully understand.

Intuition feels different for many people. For some people it can literally be a gut feeling. For others, it is a tingling of knowing in the body. It can be felt in your heart or it can be a voice inside. It often appears as a first instinct, and because of that our minds can jump in and disrupt that knowing. The mind tries to rationalize our intuition; it tries to gain control by listing off all the 'logical' reasons to ignore our intuitions.

Allow yourself time to connect to your intuition. This may be a new idea for you, or something you have been working with for a while. In either case, you will need time to connect to the quiet inner voice and time to learn to listen to it. To understand when it is speaking to you and to stop brushing past it. To trust when you want to push toward more logical answers. Be kind to yourself, as you will make mistakes. You will veer off course. It is part of getting to know yourself better.

You will find that building a steady relationship with your intuition will help you trust yourself. Be gentle and remain open to the instincts that come up. It will create more ease within because you will understand yourself; even when things don't make sense, you will know that your gut is guiding you in the direction you need to go.

# 47

# When Loneliness Takes Over

Loneliness, the only thing I am afraid of.
Unknown

Loneliness. Even the word is incredibly lonely. We **all** have lonely times in our lives. We will **all** feel alone in the world at some point. One of the darkest places we can go in our mind and body is into the darkness that loneliness can bring. It often feels part of the outer world, but it is about our inner world, and what is happening in our mind and body.

When I fall into the experience of feeling lonely, I get lonelier. Within the loneliness there is more loneliness. It creates more suffering and pain. For so many of us, being alone and quiet with our thoughts is like a war zone. It's so terrifying that we will do anything to avoid our thoughts. They feels like a bad neighbourhood full of danger and destruction.

Loneliness can come when you have not created enough time to be quiet and alone. It can come from a devastating loss, or from not having endless texts or messages come in on your phone.

We have skillfully learned to numb our feelings by choosing behaviours that distract us from our most intimate places within. We watch Netflix, we fidget around the house, we distract ourselves with kids, family and friends; we are constantly moving, always planning, creating to-do lists and so forth. We lose touch with ourselves, and this is an experience that feels off balance. Yet we know that being still with ourselves feels scarier than indulging in our distractions, so we chose what is easier, but not better.

What happens to our inner framework is that our mind and body start to get agitated. We feel more and more uncomfortable, and we need to fill our lives with more and more distracting behavior so we don't have to deal with the pain that loneliness can bring. At some point, inevitably, something happens that stops us from being able to choose those distracting behaviors. Maybe it's an injury, an illness, job loss, the death of someone close to us or a desperate need to slow down. Perhaps it is meeting someone whose life clearly brings them peace; you can feel their calmness and you desperately want that same experience. Whatever it is, it always comes. We have our moments of awakening, and in those moments, we can feel profoundly lonely. If we don't know who we are anymore, then where do we go from there?

Feeling lonely is about the fear we have. The fear of not being liked or loved, the fear of failing, the fear of things not going the way we want. The only way to combat loneliness and the inner writhing that comes from it is to show up for ourselves. We need to teach ourselves that we are here and that we can trust ourselves to show up and be present so we can move through the pain. We get pushed to do our work.

It is work; life is work. I don't mean that you have to suffer, but you do have to **show up**. If we can focus on "making our hearts a zone of peace" (Jack Kornfield), we can step out of our own judgment and find a place of peace within. It will change you, physiologically. It is impossible to hold opposites with the same intensity, so if we are able to hold peace strongly we are unable to hold the feeling of loneliness so intensely.

Find ways to show up for yourself:

1) Don't believe everything you think.
2) Surround yourself with kind people (you can just start with one kind person).
3) As a practice, slow down and be with yourself.
4) Get quiet for at least five minutes every day.
5) Watch all the ways you judge yourself. Within that watching, **don't judge** yourself. Find kind and loving ways to speak to yourself.

Most importantly, when you feel really lonely, the kind of loneliness that is dark and scary, reach out. Ask for support from your friends and family. Tell them you are struggling and that you need company. You will need them to show up and help you regain some light. This, my friend, is the most important practice.

Let us remember that when we are feeling most alone, there are many other people who are also feeling lonely. They may need us to reach out to them.

# 48

# Going with the Flow Makes Life Easier

I equate ego with trying to figure everything
out instead of going with the flow.
Pema Chodron

Ever feel like you are working so hard to make
things work? That no matter what you do, you
meet resistance or have to fight for what you want?
Do you find yourself questioning why things must be
so difficult? Or why things can't come to you as easily
as they seem to come to everyone else? Do you wonder
why you feel so tired and exhausted all the time? Or
why it feels like you are meeting conflict after conflict?

I have spent my whole life feeling these things. Trying to make things work, pushing when I could have softened. I have forced things when perhaps acceptance would have brought me more ease. I make things happen because I am capable and strong and can deal with anything that comes my way. Many of us are this way.

Recently, I have started to wonder why I'm pushing so much. I am not saying that there aren't challenges in life, but if you ever feel like it's always challenging, it is time to look at how you interact with the world.

*I was going against the flow.*

Are you making things easier, or pushing into walls? Are you not stopping until you get some kind of result?

Years ago, working on a river in the Yukon, it dawned on me that a river is an endless metaphor for life. Water flows on the path of least resistance. It moves with a grace and smoothness that is mesmerizing. When the river meets challenges – anything that blocks the path of fluidity – there is whitewater. It's a churning, loud, dangerous and challenging path if you decide to go down it. But if you find ways to navigate it, using the strength of the water – instead of pushing against it – it can be encouraging, fun and rewarding. Using the path of least resistance leads to a feeling of success.

However, if you ever try to travel up river, you quickly discover it's freaking hard. It pushes on you. You can't use the force of the river to make things easier or help you navigate. You are literally pushing against the flow.

That was what I was doing. I was constantly pushing against the flow for many personal reasons. It's taken me almost four decades to see that I wasn't flowing.

What does it mean to go with the flow? It means doing things that you **want** to be doing. It feels easier, it feels fulfilling, and it actually feels like you are gathering energy instead of flushing it down the drain. When you **go with the flow**, you stop pushing away your dreams, your desires and divine needs. You begin to listen to your heart over your head.

When we go against the flow it is often because we need to be in control, need to be in charge or want to look like we are winning all the time. We are certainly not wanting to fail in anyway. We are holding on tightly to the insecure parts of ourselves, but moving from this place creates resistance. Eventually we don't even know what makes us feel good because we are so used to pushing against...well, most things.

I heard Pema Chodron in an interview remind us, "I equate ego with trying to figure everything out instead of going with the flow".

I've discovered that if I ask myself these four questions, I can figure out if I am pushing against or moving with the flow:

1) Does this feel like expansion or contraction?
2) What is your heart saying vs. your head?

3) What excuses are you making, and why?
4) How can I make this easier?

In order to achieve genuine peace, surrender is necessary. You must become discerning to see where in your life you can let go. Do less. Trust the greater force guiding you to get you to where you are meant to be.

I now say to myself, as a mantra, and as a reminder, *If it doesn't feel easy and doesn't flow, it doesn't go.*

# 49

## What Does It Mean To 'Be Conscious'?

Choose and direct yourself to be
peaceful on the inside, regardless of
what is happening on the outside.
Unknown

'Being conscious' is a phrase on the lips of many modern, spiritual and mindful people these days. Often, when we wake up to the greater world around us and notice the larger philosophical and spiritual thoughts of today and the past, it provokes an open-eyed response. We consider ideas and concepts about ourselves that we have never explored. We start to see cause and effect and notice how we think and how we respond. We begin to see that there is a corresponding outcome. For better or worse.

When we begin to awaken, there can be a sense of accomplishment, as though we've gained passage into the world of an elite mindful. It can feel like a privilege, generating feelings of (hard-earned) superiority over those not yet on an enlightened path.

My perception of consciousness is constantly unfolding. I discuss it in all my yoga classes as well as in my business and in my coaching. There are ways in which we can wake up to ourselves. Recently, I heard Tara Brach define it like this: "Consciousness means that you have choice". It was so simple, articulate and accurate. I humbly use her teachings here.

Having consciousness means we have choice. We have the choice to get caught in our own self-defeating inner chatter, we have choice in the way we speak to other people, we have choice in how loving or kind we are to others and we have choice in how generous we are. We can choose which thoughts we indulge in, and we can choose whether we get sucked into the drama of those around us. We can choose to allow the weather to determine our happiness. We have choice in how we respond to **any** situation that lands in front of us, regardless of how difficult. We have a choice to use our pains as a rite of passage to justify our behavior. We have a choice to find ways to use our biggest challenges to move us to bigger and greater experiences.

Realizing that consciousness is about the ability to choose in any given moment, and decide who and how we want to be, is the greatest gift of being human. It is also a challenging and continuous practice that remains with us until we die.

How are you going to choose today? What moments are you going to choose to be present in? What reactive states are you ready to change? Who do you want to be in this lifetime? Now is the time to make these choices, not tomorrow, not next year, but today.

# 50

# I Am Afraid of Being Judged

Bravery is acknowledging your
fear, and doing it anyway.
Cheryl Strayed

I have **big** fears. They revolve around being judged and failing, but I haven't let them stop me from pushing myself to do some pretty incredible things in my life, things I am proud of. However, for a long time I held myself back in many ways: I was scared of putting myself out there, of failing, and of being thought a fool. Eventually, I got bored of holding myself back, and the desire to step into things I wanted to do pushed me out of my fear. I knew I needed to push myself because I was starting to feel smothered by my own insecurity.

We are all afraid of being judged.

When I started writing my Mindful Monday blog, I was scared as hell of what people would say. But I realized that my desire to remain small because of fear was getting really boring. I dug in and found the courage to just step into it. I have received lots of incredible and heartfelt feedback, but I have also received aggressive and unsupported responses. You know what? Those who don't love what I do are actually no concern of mine. I let those comments float off my back because I am in love with what I am doing. It comes from a kind place inside me. I feel comforted and pushed to try things, to get uncomfortable, and to take steps. These steps change and evolve as I explore one dream at a time.

I realized that the idea of never following my dreams was more terrifying than living a life without risk. To come to the end, whether it be tomorrow or 40 years from now, if I had never tried to do the things I dreamed of, I would feel like I had failed this life. That isn't how I want to experience this one precious life of mine.

I also realize that I will fail, but that failure isn't a negative thing. It is only scary in our minds. In reality, failure is the biggest teacher. In the moment of failing, it can feel awful, but I have learned **more** from my failures than from my successes.

"Be about 10 times more magnanimous than you believe yourself capable of being. Your life will be 100 times better for it" ~ Cheryl Strayed

What are you holding yourself back from? What are you scared of being judged for? Let's get real. It's totally intimidating to put yourself out there and do something you have never done before. It can be really scary to follow a big dream or take a risk. But what is worse: to have never tried, or to have tried and failed? Nothing ventured, nothing gained.

May we all find the courage to blow past our own limiting thoughts.

# 51

## Being Honest

Honesty is the first chapter
in the book of wisdom.
Thomas Jefferson

What is honesty to you? Seriously. Have a think on this. Are you being honest with yourself? I mean, let's be clear here: if we are going to be honest in the world, it starts with being truthful with ourselves.

I now think of honesty more simply, how I can tell myself little white lies, like it is OK that someone is treating me in a way I don't want because I know they are struggling. I tell myself that, because for some reason I am scared to lose that relationship so I avoid speaking my truth. Another example of a little while lie: a friend asks me to go for a run in the morning, but I want to want to sleep in. Instead of admitting that I am tired, I tell them that I have to work. When I start to unpack the small untruths I tell throughout my days, I am able to see how they can play into a lack of honesty with myself.

I recall when I first had my daughter: I was seriously sleep deprived and dealing with postpartum anxiety. Basically, I was a hot mess. I could barely hold conversations, let alone think straight. I knew one thing for sure: the 'mom' friends I surrounded myself with needed to be honest and upfront. Some of the moms I knew would respond with a (desperate) high-pitched "I'm great" whenever they were asked how they were doing. They were basically closing the door on any conversation about what was **really** going on for them. They became the women and mothers I couldn't be around. I needed honesty. It was too brutal for me as a new mom to pretend that everything was OK, because it absolutely wasn't.

I was being honest with myself then. But if am being honest with myself now, I am still learning to be more clear, open and forthright. I continue to offer myself to work, projects, events and people that don't feel right. I have a tendency to disconnect from the part of myself that knows better. It does not mean that those people, work, projects and events are not great; they are just not great for me right now.

I still attach to my ego and allow my ego-based insecurities to direct my decision making. But when

I listen to my inner wisdom it can save me from my desire to be liked, right or perceived as kind and open. Using insecurities as guidance never ends well. As soon as I recognize that my self-doubt is directing me, I am more capable of making intelligent choices. This is the first step in being honest: be willing to look at why you **really** do (or want to do) the things you do.

If you are lonely, learn to recognize that you are lonely. You will be able to see that the decisions you make are based on that emotion. The same theory works if you are in pain, sad, depressed or angry. Or even if you are struggling with the same conflicts repeatedly. If you are unhappy in your job or with your partner, it's time to be honest with yourself; we can't change anything in our lives until we are willing to look at and listen to ourselves with the same kind of attention we devote to the world outside of us. If we constantly place blame externally, we are living in disillusionment. We create what we experience.

When we are honest we can seek support, so be honest about the stories you tell yourself. Watch all the stories that float in your mind, and notice how you'll want to make those true by aligning your decisions with them.

Honesty brings inner peace, calm, deeper friendships and deeper connections with our partners as well as the sensation of being grounded.

Honesty and truthfulness is a lifelong investment in self.

## 52
## Learning to Say "I'm Sorry"

Saying sorry is medicine for taming our egos.

One of my biggest weaknesses has been my inability to say I am sorry. Even today, I am not professing to have mastered the art of apology, or of knowing when an apology is needed.

The art of saying sorry shifts from situation to situation.

Saying sorry isn't an answer or a cure to **all** challenging relationships or interpersonal dynamics. Saying sorry does not solve all the problems in the world. However, it does make us more accountable for our own actions and, in turn, allows us to speak and behave with consciousness. That **does** change the world.

Apologizing is a humbling action, especially if our behaviours or words have been wild and messy. Or if we really wanted to be right. I get in my own way with that one; my need to be right can blind me to the bigger picture. When I understand that if I am not right, my world will not fall apart, I take some of the aggression out of my conviction. If I can soften to other possibilities, I can choose to be compassionate toward someone else's perspective. This is a kinder response than holding my ground without compromise.

I also have a tendency to believe that everything is my fault, and this is one of the reasons it has felt so challenging to say I'm sorry. If everything is my fault, I believe I must be a horrible person; if I apologize, it makes this belief real. That's a heavy way to see the world, and it doesn't serve me. I am learning to be softer with myself and believe that I (like everyone else!) am also doing the best I can.

Sometimes things **are** my fault, but not always. When I'm not at fault, I don't have to prove my innocence: sometimes creating space for another to express themselves or better understand a situation can be a peace offering.

I am learning to say sorry to myself for my poor decisions, for being vulnerable and getting hurt, for trusting the wrong people, for not trusting myself and for not showing up as my best self. I am finding that the more I learn to forgive myself, the easier it is to forgive others. For both small and great wrongs.

Are you willing to forgive yourself above all else? What are you willing to apologize for?

# 53

# Do You Believe You Deserve Your Dreams?

Follow your dreams, they know the way.
Unknown

With all the privileges we have, especially in the Western world, we can become a bit numb to all the opportunities available to us.

First of all, have you established what it is that you want? I mean in the bigger picture. Relationships, career, children, houses, vehicles, vacations, friends, health, financial stability. The moment I started to look at my thoughts on these topics was the moment I started to wake up to what I believed I deserved.

Never questioning what I believed I deserved led me to create the unconscious beliefs that floated carelessly in my mind. Whether they were instilled socially or by my family and friends, I had taken on ideas of what I thought I deserved, and frankly, they were pretty meagre. It turns out that when I started to unpack what I thought I wanted and deserved, I had low expectations for myself.

Then I went through a stage of believing that those who wanted or accomplished big things for themselves were either a) lucky, b) better than me or c) evil (because those who covet large financial gain are clearly not spiritual).

I decided I needed to get clear on what I wanted for myself. I let my imagination go wild with possibility. When limiting stories would pop up, I would remind myself that I was capable of dreaming anything I wanted, and that the first step was to **imagine** how I wanted my life to look. I began to understand that everything I had already created in my life was from a place of dreaming my thoughts into reality, good or bad, so I better get really clear on how I want my future to look.

Being discerning with your thoughts is tremendously important to facilitating a life you want. Do you believe you deserve what you want? If not what do you believe?

Do you say things like, "I'll end up failing anyway", "I don't deserve that", "I am not worthy of love because I have too many faults", "I am not smart/skilled/ talented enough", "I want children but I wouldn't be a good parent", "I'll never find the perfect partner to parent with" or "I have to do everything on my own because no one else does it well enough"? I imagine you understand my point. There is an endless list of undeserving thoughts that keep us from achieving our potential.

The antidote? Start believing in your own dreams. I have become my own cheerleader; I constantly encourage and remind myself that I am my own best support. When I am rejected for a job or by a partner, when I fail in business or investments, these are not signs that I should give up. They are signs that I need to advocate for myself even more. If I feel a deep longing for what I want to achieve, create or experience, I am the only one who can make these things happen. It's an important practice to allow rejection to strengthen your resolve in achieve the things you want in your life instead of using it as an excuse to give up.

Make a change today. Write down all the things you have wanted in life, and then write down the thought that comes to mind often when you think of that goal. Is it a supportive thought, or is it belittling and negative? If you find that your self talk keeps you from achieving your dreams, imagine how you would want someone to encourage you, and change the next thought to one that supports your initial desire. I continue to do this practice because, as years go by, my dreams evolve with my experiences, achievements and failures. I keep revisiting the ways I hold myself back so that I can remain a positive agent of creation in my own life.

I believe you can do the same! Become your own biggest supporter.

# 54

## It's Ok Not to Be Ok

Sometimes when I say 'I'm OK', I want
someone to look at me in the eyes, hug
me tight, and say 'I know you are not'.
Unknown

I am pretty sure we all have dark thoughts at one
point or another. Like you've wandered into a tunnel
and can't see the light. It feels dark and lonely, as
though you're being swallowed up by the thoughts in
your mind.

Sometimes my head is like a bad neighbourhood that
you wouldn't want to wander into at night. There is
potential for a knife fight, or to be kidnapped and

shoved into a dark space where you may never be rescued.

When my mind wanders into unwelcome territories, I know it's time to do my work. I need to dig into my toolkit and find a lifeline to a more comfortable zone. If you don't have a toolkit, here are some ways to create one:

- Find a 'go to' friend (or friends) that you can call on when things feel desperate. Someone that you can confide in and trust. Let them know you feel dark, and that you just need someone to talk to who will listen and be supportive. I have and I have friends who, when they have gone into that deep dark neighbourhood of their minds, have called people they trust to come and be with them, to sleep beside them, to hold them because they know that, in that moment, they are incapable of holding themselves or trusting themselves.
- Get outside. Move, feel the fresh air, walk, run, hike, bike, breath deep and break a sweat. Do whatever it is that feeds you when you are connecting with nature.
- Watch funny TV shows or films. Keep it light. Avoid the temptation to indulge in entertainment that builds on your despair.
- Dance. For goodness sake, just dance! By yourself or with friends. Play your favorite upbeat song, and if you need to fake it, then fake it until you feel something lighten on the inside.

- Be of service to someone else that needs help. This is such an important act. The moment you stop giving all your attention to your own plight you will be able to open up and see the greater world. Hopefully you will see how you can improve it.
- Go see your doctor or better yet mental health practitioner. If you are feeling like none of these things are working, get yourself to the nearest doctor and ask/cry/beg for help.

It can feel like these feelings will last forever. Darkness is like that; it tends to blind us from truth and disconnect us from our light. Remember that this too shall pass. Eventually you will begin to feel lighter. Keep reminding yourself of that.

Remember that when we look at someone we often see what they want us to see. Maybe they are projecting that they have it all figured out. Perhaps we assume that success in life sets us up for a life without struggle. Remember that our assumptions that someone is 'strong' or 'capable', or our thoughts that they have nothing to be sad about are incredibly narrow minded. These are limiting thoughts and ideas that create separation instead of connection.

Ultimately, it's important to remember it is OK not to be OK. It's OK to be dealing with something that feels too big to deal with on your own. It is OK to lean on those that make you feel comfortable.

Remember, you are **not** your thoughts. I know this is hard to remember when thoughts have dictated almost all the ways we interact in the world. But trust me, you are so much greater than your thoughts would lead you to believe.

You are capable of great things, including changing your emotional state. Learn to trust that knowledge, and it will change your life.

"People who need help often don't look like those that do" Glennon Doyle

# 55

## You Are Enough

Note to self, 'You Are Enough'.

E nough. You are enough. Seriously: who you are in this moment is enough.

You do not need to be any smarter, better, skinnier, stronger, healthier, funnier, more likable, more connected, better known, more social or anything else that is taking up space in your mind.

One of my mantras is, simply, 'Enough'. I repeat it to myself over and over to remind myself that I am enough as I am.

It is not coming from the perspective that enough is enough, but from a place in me that can be incredibly mean and wants to compare myself to others or to the past or to the idea that I am not enough. So, I just say, 'Enough'. I have enough time. Enough success. Enough friends. Enough social invites. Enough love. Enough laughter. Enough smiles. Enough opportunities. Enough of everything.

As soon as I do that, I am more capable of enjoying each moment. I let go of the indulgent side of me that wants more, that indulges in the shitty feelings that I, well, indulge in.

I am enough. You are enough. We are enough.

It doesn't mean we aren't conscious. It means we are enough within our own lives. From the place of 'enough' it is easier to access opportunities simply because we are not coming from a place of lack. This means that there is less time to indulge in unpleasant feelings and more time to just enjoy life.

You are enough.

# 56
## Are Your Excuses Holding You Back?

The only person who is truly holding you back is you. No more excuses. It's time to change. It's time to live life at a new level.
Tony Robbins

We all get in our own way. We have excuses for why we choose not to ask someone on a date, apply for a job, move, have kids, take a vacation, end a bad relationship, have a relationship, save money, write that book, make the most of weekends, make happiness a priority or have that difficult conversation.

Excuses bog down our lives. They become our biggest limitations. They encourage us to stay small. They help us avoid taking risks. They keep us in our comfort zones. Sometimes we even place our excuses on others so we don't have to own them. Our excuses help define our lives in a way that limits our potential.

Our reasons for our excuses can become so ingrained in our way of interacting with the world – and in our minds – that we don't even notice that we have allowed them to control our lives. I find the best way to identify my excuses is to watch them as they feed into my mind or out of my mouth. Once I catch an excuse, I can start to follow its path. Why did I use that excuse? How does that excuse prevent me from doing x, y or z? Once I identify an excuse, I can then recognize it for what it is: an excuse.

This awareness allows me to step outside of the safety that the excuse provides. It doesn't have to be my truth just because I have said it or believed it. I can experiment with my perceived boundaries and limitations, and I can expand my reach beyond what I have seen as 'safe'. It is an amazing thing to watch yourself transition through life.

What are your excuses? What are you willing to change so that those excuses are no longer your truths?

# 57

# Be Different, It's Worth It

Don't be afraid of being different, be afraid
of being the same as everyone else.
Unknown

D o you feel like you need to fit in with the crowd?
Do what others do, dress as others do, do work
that others approve of, date a certain kind of person?
Do you prefer being a rule follower so that your friends,
family and neighbors don't judge you? Or do you just
want to be liked so much that you will sacrifice your
own ideas, dreams and passions for others' approval?

God forbid that we are disliked.

The people in the world who are making big and small change in business, life, love and family do one thing that other people don't. Do you know what that is? They don't care that they are different or have different ideas. They play by their own rules and do not subscribe to the idea that they should fit in above all else.

Since I was young, I have been told by friends and family that I should be a certain way. Society teaches us as children that we should be good girls and boys, that we should avoid being perceived as 'bad' at all cost. If you choose to be different, you can be cast out, bullied or gossiped about. It happens to adults as well.

As a business owner, I am constantly being judged about what I should or should not be doing. If I paid attention to all that, I would just be spinning in a world of 'shoulds' in order to be liked. The thing is, I just don't freaking care! It's not that I don't care about people: I care deeply about others. I am called to be of service. I will show up for anyone who asks me, but I won't do things just because other people think I should. As I become more focused on pursuing my own goals, I am getting better and better at cutting out the distraction of others' unsolicited opinions and advice. In doing so, I am feeling happy and whole and inspired in my own life.

We are not taught how to forge our own paths, how to go against the grain, how to follow our own passions or desires or how to do what lights us up. Everybody has opinions about what we should wear, what we should consume, who we should hang out with or even what we should aspire to in our careers. I am so over it. I am over being someone else for other people. Over the past three or so years, I have come to understand how I have limited my life because I didn't want to be different or judged. It's not that I no longer have insecurities or doubts, but I am no longer motivated by a desire to fit in. I would rather just be me.

Allow your own uniqueness to shine. Be who you want to be. Strive for the life **you** want and not for what others want for you or want you to be. Get your **freak** on if you that's what really lights you up. Dive into the great unknown of yourself and see what shows up. If there are people in your life that are going to judge you for being different than they would like, so be it. That is about them, not about you. Once you start to understand that no one else decides how best to be you, it will be easier to find, celebrate and use your strengths and gifts.

Please! Go be (amazing) you.

# 58

# Have You Allowed Your Heart to Break?

Don't be afraid to be the one
that loves the most.
Unknown

The fear that comes with having our heart broken is what holds us back from living a full life. Our fears can stop us from building connections and taking risks. They can make us cold, cynical and self-protective. Pain can be a weapon when we find ourselves making sure we hurt others before they hurt us. Most of this is unconscious behaviour, which is likely why it is still happening.

Heartbreak comes from many places: from losing a loved one, from being disrespected by a friend, from having failed in a business endeavor or from losing a job. It can come when a romantic relationship ends and you feel deeply wounded and unable to trust yourself. Heartbreak can come from things that are out of our control; it can also come from trauma that we have endured but have not yet found a way to heal.

Over the past decade I have experienced all the examples I listed above. One heartbreak occurred when someone I was deeply in love with suddenly and unexpectedly ended our relationship. It sent me into the darkest place I had ever experienced in my heart. It was a fast tailspin into a dark depression. It created an anxiety that made me feel like I might implode, and for a time it took everything I had to just show up in my life. Even my friends who had been happy for me were feeling disappointed and losing hope that any of us could find something healthy and loving. It was a scary time, but only one of the many heartbreaks I have experienced over my lifetime. We all have them.

Shortly after that happened, I made an oath that I would not let it break me. I chose to go deep into my own healing so that I could come out of the pain ready to open my heart again to the world. I chose to have it break me open instead of breaking me entirely. I was determined to move forward with an open heart, even if it was scary. I healed myself rather quickly because I allowed my pain to overwhelm me; I allowed myself to be in the heaviness of my sadness even when all I wanted to do was run as far away from it as possible. I was lonely, hurting and scared and I felt like I might not survive. But after years of practicing this work, I knew I needed to remain in the awful emotions. It's not that I did not feel any less awful than anyone else going through a similar situation, but I I knew that this too would shift. I would once again feel different: gentler and softer and more loving toward myself for showing up in my inner work.

When we don't allow ourselves the opportunity to hurt and break down, we stunt our growth and our hearts. We close off from developing deeper connections with others because our connection with ourselves has been closed off. We tend to project our pain toward others, to our friends and family and beyond. When someone in our circle is putting themselves out there in a way that terrifies us, we might tell them all the reasons they shouldn't do it. We can place our limitations on others and try to stunt their growth if we've limited our own. We may attach, judge, become righteous or see ourselves as better, all in order to hold onto control so we don't have to feel our own pain.

In the long run, doing this makes us lonely and can riddle us with dis-ease. We may become anxious, stressed or controlling. We might even start to micromanage our environments and feel really certain about our opinions. We may keep ourselves so busy we can barely keep up in our lives. There becomes no space for seeing things in any other ways because we are holding on so tight to our worlds, views, and opinions just to avoid feeling anything.

A lifetime of this will leave you living in a small, judgement based world. It will lead you to keep everyone out that doesn't see things the way you do, or participate in the world you the way you think they should. You may even be able to justify your judgements and feel you are blameless for your feelings and beliefs because of all the things you've endured.

This is an exhausting existence. All structured just so you don't have to feel your emotions.

I implore you to take the risk to stop, to unravel, to feel your heart ache and to allow for your pain – as uncomfortable as it is – to have space to exist. It will be one of the hardest things you do, but you will come out of it a braver, kinder and more loving version of yourself.

Want to be supported in this work?

Trust that you are supported by something greater than what you can see. That is spirituality: by learning to trust and have faith, you will be guided through the darkest nights of your life.

## 59

## Sometimes Things Just Don't Work Out

Life will give you whatever experience
is most helpful for the evolution
of your consciousness.
Eckhart Tolle

Despite all your good intentions, positive thinking and intention-setting, sometimes you are just going to fall. Or fail. Or stumble. Maybe even rumble. For reasons you can't yet understand or possibly **don't yet need** to understand, within your struggles there are likely greater lessons at hand, or greater gifts. Only time will tell.

It's not uncommon in our world of 'self-development' to believe that if we are clear, genuine and loving, if we set clear intentions, have big dreams, and don't dwell in the difficult times, that life will joylessly provide. I think that can lead us down a road of false positivity and disconnect us from reality.

So sometimes when you stumble, when things don't look the way you thought they would, it might be time to soften, cry, allow, let go, trust or maybe lean your head on a tender shoulder.

Eckhart Tolle says (in his book *A New Earth; Awakening to Your Life's Purpose*) "Life will give you whatever experience is most helpful for the evolution of your consciousness. How do you know that this is the experience that you need? Because this is the experience you have having at the moment."

You don't have to know the answers. Trusting in the unknown is a skill, and allowing ourselves to develop that skill can bring great ease.

What ways do you feel you are not getting what you want?

Can you imagine what it would be like to go with the flow and see where you end up? As one of my most cozy sweaters says, 'trust the journey'.

I am still learning to trust in the things I can't yet understand.

# 60

# Are You Giving Your Power Away?

The only keeper of your happiness is you.
Stop giving people power to control your
smile, your worth and your attitude.
Mandy Hale

You may be wondering what 'giving away your power' means.

I can give you examples of how I have done exactly this. When I become overwhelmed by fear, when I feel myself physically contract and I get lost in not knowing what to do or when I blame someone else for my own experience, I am giving away my power.

I gave away my power in my past relationship. I stayed in a relationship that didn't serve me because I did not think I had a choice. Choosing to stay left me feeling resentful, unhappy, under-stimulated, inwardly toxic and unsupported. I was scared of the unknown and because I got lost in that fear, it ate up my sense of worthiness.

I also give my power away when I get hooked on dramas, or when I choose to make a big deal about something instead of forgiving (myself) and letting it go. I give away my power when I feel self-important and think I am the only one who can fix a problem, or when my ego is wounded and I feel like the only way to recover is to prove that I am right instead of sitting in the wounded place and working on loving myself.

I lose my power when something challenging is happening in my life and I fantasize about someone else swooping in and fixing it. In fact, when I have had someone else swoop in and fix something, it has often backfired, leaving me having to solve a much larger problem. In turn, I feel more overwhelmed and stressed because of it. There is a big difference between someone helping and someone taking over a problem that needs to be solved. It's more than OK to receive help, but you must be the one who makes the decisions to best serve **you**.

**Someone helping** = being in control but being open to help and to not having all the answers.

**Someone else problem solving** = throwing up your hands and letting someone else make all the decisions, and potentially creating circumstances where you can blame someone or be blamed for the outcome.

We often give our power away in relationships. Giving over power to a partner allows us to blame them for outcomes, and to be disappointed and resentful. If we can recognize that whatever happens in the relationship, we will be OK (maybe hurt but absolutely not broken by our own choices, no matter what), then we are agents in the unfolding of whatever we create with the other people in our lives instead of waiting for our lives to happen *to* us.

Putting someone on a pedestal is another way we give away our power. No matter how perfect or capable or incredible or desirable someone else seems, we are all human and all the same at the end of the day; we are as rich with our faults as with our own gifts. Do not underestimate your own worth. Place someone higher than yourself and they will certainly fall down; likely this will be more painful for you than for them.

When we give our power away, we **suffer**. I suffer greatly when I get angry, frustrated or pissed off and respond to the world from that place. These emotions are an unavoidable part of my experience, but when I choose to respond with these emotions is when I lose balance. Giving our power away feels off balance. It is indulging in blaming. It is pointing to others for our own experiences.

How do you give away your power? Is it worth it?

If we can learn to be at peace with our own emotions, if we can learn to be at peace with our fragile hearts, if we can learn to be at peace with not knowing outcomes or the reasons why, we will stop giving away our power. We will remain open-hearted and free from suffering.

# 61

## What Would You Do if Nobody Was Watching?

Work like you don't need the money,
love like you've never been hurt,
dance like nobody's watching.
Satchel Paige

I was skilled at living my life the way I perceived other people wanted me to, how my friends and family told me I should. I did this for a lot of my life. I recall being very young and having absolute freedom. I remember feeling happiness and a sense of trust in the greater world and knowing I would be taken care of. Somewhere around age six or seven, things changed. I felt the joy leave me. I can remember starting to struggle more in school and in my home. I recall being sad. A lot. And not only sad, but frozen trying to figure out what others wanted of me instead of trying to understand what I wanted for myself.

This started the long practice of not knowing or trusting myself. I started living for others. A few things happened to cause this. My parents got a divorce, and my dad moved out. My mom struggled a lot for reasons I couldn't understand. I experienced abuse. A lot has unraveled in my life, and it began at a tender age with the awareness that I wasn't safe and the sadness that came with that. Both deeply uprooted me.

I learned that having an opinion that differs from others leads to not being worthy of friendships, love or respect. It's been painful, but I have arrived at a point where I am confident enough in myself to have my own thoughts, dreams and opinions. I can let go of doing what others think I should be doing. Whether it's who I should date or how big I can dream, choosing for myself has been – by far – the most courageous thing I have done in my life.

We all have a journey, a story, an experience or a trauma that has shifted us and changed us. We all have something that has taught us we need to respond to making others happy instead of ourselves.

Where was this moment for you? How is that story stopping you from living like no one is watching?

What are you doing for show? How are you living to please others?

Are you choosing to be around certain people because they make you fit into an image you've created? Or are you choosing people because you like them and feel full and happy when you are with them? Are you living in a house that fills you up on the inside or one that only looks good on the outside? Is your relationship/career/life the dream you always imagined (even within the struggles), or is it what you think keeps you in good social standing?

If no one was watching right now, what would you do? Would you dance? Would you change careers or start your own business? Would you travel more? Would you call that man/woman? Would you leave your relationship? Would you wear something different? How would you change the way you make decisions?

I had to have a hard look at myself, and I was living for others instead of for what actually lit me up. Not everyone around me has supported my decisions. But today, I am refining my inner need to please and to do what others think I should do. It's been a detox, this letting go of pleasing or being accepted and liked. I now move with an intention of heart and never with an intention to harm: I know I am moving from the right place, even if others don't see or understand my motives. Using this motivation keeps me accountable to the most important person in my life: myself.

The side effect is that I am far more compassionate toward others, and I am less likely to jump to conclusions.

Are you living in the fear of disapproval? Would you choose to go to an event, even if you thought your social circle wouldn't approve? How are you holding tight and not expressing yourself for fear of being judged? What are you **not** doing? What are you holding back?

Dance with life, like no one is watching. Move toward your deepest dreams. Follow the voice within that is asking to be heard. Let go, just a little, and see how it feels.

# 62

## A Love Affair Like This

Let yourself be silently drawn by the
strange pull of what you really love.
It will not lead you astray.
Rumi

I am moving into the biggest love affair of my life. It took me over 40 years to realize that this love I had been neglecting was going to be the most important love of my life.

I am in the midst of a love affair with myself. I realize I have been neglecting the most raw and precious part of myself: my heart. I thought I'd been catering to the desire for love, but I realize it had been an exterior feasting instead of an inner reclaiming.

I'm reclaiming the parts of me that know how to be patient; I'm allowing for things to not go as I planned; I'm acting with kindness and compassion. I am allowing myself to feel sexy, to be feminine, to be sweet and strong. To be quiet when I want to be loud and opinionated when I am tempted to be quiet. To be open to new experiences and to say yes to things I normally say no to and say no to things I normally say yes to. And it's really hard.

It turns out that I am impatient with myself. I have little tolerance for my mistakes or for what I perceive to be my failures. I am rugged and pushy. I expect so much. I rarely ask for help. I have a hard time leaning on others. Can you relate?

I was thirsty for romance, but I'd built a world that was on a weak foundation. I didn't believe I was worthy of having what I dreamed of. I am learning to be more accepting of myself and the days that are not so sparkly. I am learning to accept pain. I am creating space to crumble, and within that, I am learning to be tender and gentle with myself.

I want to offer these parts of myself to my future lover. I want to be kinder to myself, so I can be kinder to the one(s) I choose to be intimate with.

When we journey in relationships, we quickly realize that it is work. We must consistently choose to show up and be present and engage without throwing away something good because it becomes difficult. When we decide to create a world with another person, it takes dedication, trust and resilience. Our partners will make mistakes. We will make mistakes. At moments, some of those mistakes can feel unforgivable. Sometimes they may be unforgivable. Most of the time, though, we can dig deep enough to forgive so that we can choose to continue the journey together.

My point is, if I cannot be kind, tender, forgiving, passionate and open with myself, how can I ever give that to someone else? I realize I can't.

In this sweet, rest-of-my-life love affair, I am choosing to be aware that it takes effort to keep the passion going. I want to feel the heat of passion always. I want to feel the desire to smile at myself in the morning, to see the good in me. I want to have a healthy perspective about how I look which keeps me accountable to making healthy choices around exercise, meditation, nourishing food, loving friends, family and co-workers.

Even the act of writing this is an example of loving myself. I feel freer, more resilient and excited about what I will create next. I am curious about who I will invite into my sacred life, be it friends, family or loves. I am called to show up, to be present in many moments throughout my days and to be as loving as possible with myself.

Are you ready for your next love affair?

# 63

# How Cheap Is Your Happiness?

The art of being happy lies in the power of
extracting happiness from common things.
Henry Ward Beecher

How much do you value your happiness? Are you
willing to give it away to anyone who challenges
your ideas? Would you allow a triggering email to
dissolve a beautiful state? Are you willing to fall into
self-comparison when you go on social media, letting
your mind entertain that you are either better or worse
than what you see there?

Does the weather get to make choices for you? Do you
get frustrated when it's not glorious outside? I see this

**all** the time, people sacrificing their power to what's happening outside. What about on the inside? If your good state is dependent on something as changeable as the weather, what is happening in your inner environment? It's possible you are stirring in constant inner storms.

What if you understood that you have power over how you feel? What if you realized that the stories you tell yourself are exactly that: stories? Have you considered what it would feel like to change those stories?

Here is a five-minute practice that can help shift your attention and emotional state and let the stories subside. It is relatively easy to do at work, home, in your car (keeping your eyes open if you're driving), on a walk or while you are making dinner. All you really need is a couple of minutes to get quiet.

Close your eyes, deepen your breathing and draw your attention to the centre of your chest. Breathe deeply into your heart space. Let your breath invoke space and a feeling of presence. Breath is the one thing that, when we focus on it, allows us to be completely present. When we focus on it, we are not in the past or the future. We are right here, in this moment. Once you have connected to your heart space, think of the simple things you are grateful for. Breathe that gratitude into your heart space. Allow the feeling to flow outward from your heart as you exhale. Continue this for several patient, conscious breathes. Notice what shifts as you experience full awareness. What changes when you step out of the suffering attached to relying on certain conditions, outcomes, validation or experiences?

I really enjoy spending time in more beautiful states.

# 64

# What Is The Ego, and How Does It Serve Us?

The ego tends to equate having with
being; I have therefore I am.
And the more I have, the more I am.
The ego lives through comparison.
How you are seen by others turns
into how you see yourself.
Eckhart Tolle

The ego, what is it? How does it serve or hinder our experiences? How can we move forward mindfully without being constantly controlled and manipulated by it?

The design and function of our ego is ancient and out of date. It serves an important role in our civilization as it keeps us on constant alert and aware of potential dangers. It was designed to keep us in our stress response – fight, flight or freeze. Because of that important function, it has allowed us to thrive and become the individuals we are today: very smart and creative problem solvers who are talented enough to create a world that has evolved into a modern and technologically-driven era.

However, I think our ego function is hindering our evolution. Because we are constantly worried and anxious, the ego hasn't developed in the same way our world has. It continues to warn us that we are unsafe and convinces us that we should respond within that framework of operation.

The ego does this by pulling us into stress in response to the events around us. It does this by dominating our mind. It is the part of us that wants to label people, experiences, thoughts and ideas. It is the part of us that separates us from love and moves us toward fear.

Micheal Beckworth says the acronym for ego is "Edging God Out" ('God' could be replaced with goodness or goddess). I love this acronym because it reminds me that when our ego is in control, we lose sight of our higher selves or the part of us that moves beyond reactivity. The ego removes our capacity to be kinder to ourselves or others. There is always a motive associated with the ego.

How do you establish whether you are moving from ego, or from a place of awareness? Ego tends to be that place within us that is pushing against goodness, the part that convinces us to be on high alert and dismantles our sense of well-being. It is from this place that we are driven to fight; the ego tells us that our thoughts are real and we will be safe if we continue to believe these thoughts. I believe, however, that when we can connect to the intelligence of our bodies and to the wisdom of sensation, and when we learn to override the system within us that feels scared or fearful, we will reach far greater peace in our internal and external worlds.

I really like what Eckhart Tolle has to say about how to know when we are disconnecting from our egos: It is when we reach a place where we recognize our thoughts, and our attachment to our thoughts, that we are able to question our desire to make those thoughts a reality. It is when we simply stop and observe instead of reacting and conforming to those thoughts. In that moment we have disempowered our ego.

It has become a steady practice for me to allow my ego to be less involved in my decision making. I work at letting go of labeling people. I work on controlling my desire to react. I am learning to resist the temptation to react and label a situation. It is big work for me, but through it I experience far less inner conflict and fewer dramas in my life.

Here is an example of how I put this into practice: When I have had my heart 'crushed' by a lover who didn't behave in a way I wanted them to, as efficiently as I can, I work to let go of making this other person into a 'bad guy'. Their actions may not have been kind, but the more I hold onto the story of hating them or making them bad, the longer it takes for me to recover. Some people assume I am disconnecting and avoiding my feelings with this practice, but I can assure you this is not the case. I still allow myself to feel, whether it is anger, hurt or frustration, but I no longer allow the emotions to take over my world indefinitely. I let go so I can release the pain and become more beautifully connected with myself and the world around me.

The ego is a big teacher. When we soften our attachment to it, we move into a more loving state. We no longer feel that we are constantly under assault. When we let go of that, we no longer (unconsciously or consciously) feel like we are self-protecting and we can be freer in the world. With that freedom we can access our playfulness, our kindness, our compassion, our sense of ease and our overall sense of lightness.

Trust the journey

# 65

# Trust the Things You Can't Explain

Faith is to believe in what you
do not see, the reward of faith is
to believe in what you see.
Saint Augustine

From what I witness, humans have a strong need
for certainty. Generally, we want to know what's
coming, and we want to have control. In order to have
control, we need to know that things will come to
fruition based on the way we have them mapped out
in our minds. When that happens, we feel delight,
satisfaction and mastery over our plan. It feels like
we are in control of ourselves and our inner and outer

environments, and goodness, that does feel great. Everything is moving predictably and as it should.

When my life feels easy, everything is going as planned and I alone get to make my decisions. It is rewarding just to live in that flow. However, when something finally breaks the flow, and I am no longer the decision maker, I can get immediately frustrated and manufacture a story about why I have lost control and how that is wrong.

Over the past decade, I have become more curious about this need for control in myself and others. I've watched the controlling tendencies of those around me, and I have witnessed my own need for control as it ebbs and flows over the years. We become more of what we place our attention on. We become more of that part of ourselves as we age because we continue to reinforce that behavior within ourselves.

The thing is that when we **need** to control in such a (perhaps) compulsive manner, we decrease our potential for new experiences. We begin to make our world smaller and inaccessible to others. We'll hold so tightly that we no longer enjoy our day to day life, because opening ourselves up to enjoyment means embracing uncertainty and new experiences. We move forward with caution, so that nothing, or almost nothing, will disrupt our well-organized sense of control. It starts to become confining, and we have less opportunity for any kind intimacy because intimacy requires letting go. We lack ease and openness. We lack the ability to go with the flow.

If we are letting our controlling mind rule our experience, when something happens over which we have no control and we feel surprised by the situation, this presents an opportunity to exercise even more control. We may do that by removing choices – for response or action – from ourselves or those around us. We may choose to decrease our exposure to unexpected or unpredictable outcomes. We may stop being able to cope altogether, throwing our hands up in rage or disengaging completely to avoid facing the knowledge that we can't ever be in charge of every possible thing in our lives.

If you want to create space for new experiences, you need to lean into the universe and trust something greater than you will have your best interests in mind. Plan and know what you'd like to experience but allow that the plan may not go as you hope. Detours, unexpected roads and stops along the way are what make your life richer and more colourful. See what happens to your body when you stop holding the steering wheel of your life so tightly. You'll notice that you open up: your jaw softens, your lips become more supple and your eyes open wider. Curiosity takes over need. You begin to dance in the duality within, appreciating the difference between the part of you that wants certainty and the part that is willing to see the magic that lies ahead.

My 6-year-old daughter often asks for magic, and I explain to her that magic comes in those moments of the unexpected, when something special happens you haven't planned for. She doesn't really get it, because she wants to fly, and it's hard to explain that magic is not about flying, but allowing for the things you can't explain.

There is ease in allowing for the things you can't explain or haven't planned. Some call the unexplained magic, some call it the divine, others call it God and there are those who refer to it as luck. It doesn't matter what you want to call it. What matters is the space you give yourself from a desire to control, from a desired outcome. If you just let the reins go a little, just a little, and allow for new experiences, unexpected conversations, or the possibility of saying yes to something you never imagined saying yes to, there is magic to be found. Especially in the moments you are unable to explain.

It is not a decision you make to suddenly find yourself free of your desire to control. It is the moments that you can stop, catch yourself and release a little tension from your body. The moments you exhale deeply enough to feel your body soften.

In that moment you will find something shift within you that is nothing you could have imagined before.

May we all find the power within to let go, just a little, today.

# 66

# How Our Strong Attachments Make Us Unhappy

According to Buddhist psychology, most of our troubles stem from attachment to things we mistakenly see as important.
Dalai Lama

Strong attachments. We all have them. We get attached to ideas, to people, to things and to outcomes. We often structure our lives around our attachments. They become our anchor to who we believe we are. They give us a sense of purpose and meaning in our lives – but is that what they are actually providing? Meaning and purpose?

Let me put it this way: over the last few years I have begun to question why I think and believe the things or stories that I tell myself. I do this because I started to recognize that what I was telling myself often wasn't serving me. In fact, I found that the attachments I had been developing to my beliefs started to limit the amount of joy that I was experiencing in my life.

I have a couple of examples which give context to what I mean. My first story is about the attachment I had to a house. A house of my own. I have purchased three homes in my life, but at some point I began to equate my ability to create a comfortable life with my ability to own a home. It had become an attachment. When my marriage ended, we sold the house we had purchased only 18 months earlier. It was really sad, and as we moved through our separation, I kept trying to find ways to keep the house. I had become really attached to the house. It was a dream house of sorts, and I felt that letting go of it was moving backwards. But in the end, because of extenuating circumstances, I let my house go.

One of the reasons I was able to let it go was because I had invested in another property with a friend. It was perfect, if you equate perfection with outside accomplishments, or if you value stuff as something that brings comfort, which at the time I did. We purchased the house, but it all ended up being a nightmare. There were issues with building, but a much larger implosion of issues landed me in court twice and affected some of my financial stability. In the end, I lost money.

I have since sold the place, but in the process I learned that I care more about my home being a place that does not cause me stress. Home is what I make it – it does not make me. Being happy directly correlates with feeling at ease in my life. I have also learned, after renovating two houses and my business building twice, that material possessions can create a lot of stress. So I have let go of buying, renovating and acquiring (for the time being) in order to regain a sense of ease in my life. It doesn't mean I don't have dreams for my future, but my dreams aren't hinged on the expectation that my acquisitions will promote my sense of well-being.

Another example is about my attachment to outcomes, which is woven into the first example. My attachment to outcomes held me in the idea that 'stuff' would bring me what I wanted in life. My attachment to outcomes kept me in relationships that no longer served me, sometimes for way too long. It kept me in friendships, work relationships and intimate connections that were depleting and exhausting. My attachment to outcomes prevented me from feeling successful in my business if I wasn't meeting my financial goals. I was fixated on financial success instead of being driven by service and the creation of a business that filled me from the inside out. I had to let go of my attachment to how much money I wanted to make a choice in order to devote myself to work that brought me the joy of being of service.

When I chose to start writing my Mindful Mondays blog, I had to let go of the idea of how many people would read them, or the benefits I might reap. Had I not let go, I would have not gotten this far. Nor would this project of passion have ended up turning into a book. I had never imagined that at the start of this journey. Once I let go of attachments, I was able to go with the flow, follow my creative side and tap into the flow of life.

I believe being attached to outcomes drives us to deep unhappiness (even depression) and to feelings of worthlessness. It compromises our ability to follow our hearts (our true self), or Ananda (meaning our true self – our connection to a natural state of bliss, joy and happiness).

My attachment to believing that people who have the same views, lifestyles and goals in life are the ones I want to hang out with, or connect with, limits my ability to broaden my world and see other perspectives. It makes it so I think I am right and everyone who doesn't fall into my imagined world is wrong. I miss out on life when I do this.

What are your attachments? What limits you from living a life that is full of ease and connectivity to your natural state of being? Our natural state of being is to flow and feel love and joy, regardless of the challenges that are being offered.

I don't care about being liked, or whether people agree with me. I care about being courageous and I continue to have the faith to follow my heart instead of getting caught in the ring of fire my attachments can create for me. I keep getting burned there, and when that happens, I can no longer dance like nobody's watching. If someone doesn't believe in what I am doing, I am also able to avoid the temptation to buy into their attachments of who I should be. I am free to live my life and be of service to a purpose that I get glimpses of. Ultimately, I have discovered that following my heart becomes a place of space instead of a place that feels contracted and confined by outcomes.

# 67

# The Difference Between Being Broken and Being Broken Open

What if the event you thought broke you
has actually given you an opportunity to be
broken open.

It's kind of poetic, the idea of being broken. Being broken allows us to behave in certain ways – generally ways that keep us small. Being broken becomes a badge of honor that we proudly carry along with us. It feels almost righteous, like we have earned something. Broken can give us reasons to have closed perspectives, to opt out of relationships, to hide from the world, to isolate ourselves and our minds.

When we feel fractured, it can feel like we have the right to our pain and the thoughts and beliefs that feed it. Like we have earned reasons to respond to situations with excuses for our behaviors. When I am acting from a feeling of being broken, it is as if I have given myself a permission slip to be in pain, to disconnect from my heart and to separate myself from those I care about deeply.

My partner cheated on me, so I no longer trust men/women. I lost my job once and no longer feel like I am safe financially, even though I now have a steady career. I trusted someone with a secret and they didn't respect the agreement and chose to share it; I no longer trust anyone with my secrets. I am scared of being heartbroken again. I need to keep my heart closed. Sound familiar? We tell ourselves all this crazy stuff about painful events in our lives, and it stops us from feeling free; it confines us to being nothing more than broken.

Being broken gives us reason to not show up in our relationships, in our work, in our families and most importantly, in our own lives.

What if the event that you felt broke you has actually given you an opportunity to be broken open?

I once thought I was broken. It was a very dark place. I was worried for my sanity and my ability to resurface. After a week, I began by taking deep breaths, and said, "I will not be broken by this. I will allow this to open me." I didn't want it to harden and close me. I could see how I could easily allow that to happen, so I promised myself a gift: I would allow it to move me into more beautiful places within my own body. I didn't know how I would do it, but I just knew that I had to allow that to be my truth instead of the truth I wanted to indulge in, which was that I was broken.

I decided to go as fully into the pain as I could. Anytime I watched myself pull back I would then ease myself further into it. I knew that if I could step into the eye of my inner storm, the storm would settle. So, I allowed myself to feel all the pain, disappointment, anxiety, bitterness and anger. Over time (and relatively speaking, not that long), the pain subsided and it had much less hold over me. It was no longer my whole story, only part of it.

You can do this with new pain or older hurts. Instead of ignoring your feelings, allow yourself to feel the feeling until it no longer has power over you. This will be hard, because it is normally enormously intense. Find someone who can support you during this time, be it a friend or a therapist. Remember to allow yourself time to heal, time to feel dark and time, maybe, to retreat. But keep support close, so that when you need to, you can reach out, even if it is just to have someone listen to you as you unravel.

Allow your healing to be poetry instead of pain. Allow your smile to penetrate your heart, so you can see that you have been broken open to more brilliant places than you could have ever imagined. Eventually learn to see the gifts that pain offers. Make that your mission. You are so strong. Strength doesn't come from hardening, it comes from learning to soften.

# 68

## I Got Messy

Embrace the glorious mess that you are.
Elizabeth Gilbert

In the past, I have desperately wanted to hide my 'messy' self. In fact, I still want to hide her. I don't want to show how much I strive for stability by holding onto control. I am embarrassed when I fumble in social situations. When I have an outburst of anger about something or someone that has triggered me, I am super shy. I get frustrated when, caught in my shyness, I can't be as charming as I would like to be at my very public studio.

I know I'm not perfect....and doesn't everyone want me to be perfect?

Well, guess what? When I am sloppy and clumsy, it is 'real', and sometimes being real brings up uncomfortable emotions for others. Witnessing 'messy' isn't always easy, and it can feel like watching a train wreck. No one likes to watch a wreck.

I am learning to be much more forgiving of myself. To remind myself that I am working on being human, and sometimes I fall flat on my face. Sometimes I don't listen to others very well, and I even talk when my dearest friends are talking, because I get overwhelmed with my own thoughts.

What is a girl to do? Be sloppy, or be quietly perfect, and not show the world the real me? You've probably established that I have chosen to follow the messy path. The path that is awake with self-discovery and self-work sometimes looks dirty.

Who do you want to please? Do you want to please the outside world more than your inner world? Maybe the question is, why do you want people to think you have it all sorted out? Why do you feel so dysfunctional when you are feeling all the emotions? Who in your life is rejecting the sloppy you?

To be clear, I am not advocating existing in a sloppy, unconscious state. What I am asking is, what do you prioritize? Do you put on a mask so you won't be judged, or do you remove your mask, and be real?

Are you able to embrace all the parts that make you 'You'? Are you able to show yourself around those you supposedly trust, those you collect in your inner circle?

What about not caring what other people think? Would that be possible, in a world that has become dominated by social media and outward appearances? In a world where speaking your truth doesn't always lead to the 'right' outcomes? Where there's a very real chance you will be judged?

It takes a solid inner foundation to not care what others think, and to care about what you think. That, my friend, is the big work. It is the measure of success. It is the ability to be at peace with your truth and tap into your own inner well-being, instead of waiting for others to stabilize you with their approval. It seems that anyone can become famous these days. Many people have become incredibly successful in their work. But the ability to find comfort in your mess will outlast any outward success or praise.

So, the question is, are you ready to embrace your messy self?

# 69
## Prayer

Be present and awake to the gifts of being
alive, in this moment, today.

This week is about prayer for me. I am called to
remember what is important beyond my need to
control outcomes and to trust in a bigger truth. This is
a prayer for myself and all of us as we venture in our
lives – both in times of ease or deep pain:

*Love today - find the fullest expression of love in
everything you do.*

*Embrace moments, breathe with a quality of presence
that requires a solid devotion to wanting to endlessly
taste life.*

*Be present and awake to the gifts of being alive, in this moment, today.*

*Be curious about your breath; follow it. Offer it more respect and devotion.*

*Care enough about being human to do your inner work. Never settle with yourself. Be kind yet curious enough to continuously become a more conscious version of yourself, without judgment of yourself or of others.*

*Question why you do the things you do, and why you react the way you do.*

*Do this daily: hands to your heart and breathe.*

*As my daughter volunteered at the age of four, with wisdom beyond her years, LOVE IS TRUTH!*

*Find a way to love yourself with courage. To feel the light within you expand.*

*Embrace the things you do not know or understand. Find stillness in the unknown and then go deeper until you find bliss.*

*Find your wild side, take yourself out of your comfort zone and look at life with curiosity.*

*Without thinking, try new things.*

*Don't settle in what is. Be inspired to search beyond the mediocre.*

*Know that we are **all** fragile and that we all want to be heard and acknowledged.*

*Give without wanting in return. Want more love, give more love. Want more excitement, be more exciting. Want more friends, show up more for the friends you already love.*

Printed in the United States
By Bookmasters